TEACHER'S JOKE AND STORY BOOK

**"Full well they laughed
with counterfeited glee at all his jokes, for
many a joke had he."**

(Oliver Goldsmith - 1728 - 1774)

COLLECTED by
STANLEY B. GRAHAM

AuthorHouse™
1663 Liberty Drive
Bloomington, IN 47403
www.authorhouse.com
Phone: 1 (800) 839-8640

No part of this book may be reproduced, stored in a retrieval system, or transmitted by any means without the written permission of the author.

Published by AuthorHouse 06/14/2016

ISBN: 978-1-5246-0952-8 (sc)
ISBN: 978-1-5246-0951-1 (e)

Library of Congress Control Number: 2016908231

Print information available on the last page.

Any people depicted in stock imagery provided by Thinkstock are models, and such images are being used for illustrative purposes only. Certain stock imagery © Thinkstock.

This book is printed on acid-free paper.

Dedicated to the memories of

Cynthia Ann Davis Graham (1933-1991)

And

Elizabeth "Betty" Menges Ramirez Graham

(1920-2009)

Who endured these jokes,

Enjoyed most of them,

Memorized the punch lines,

Encouraged to tell them,

And to compile them in this book.

PREFACE

TEACHER'S JOKE AND STORY BOOK

My original purpose in compiling these jokes was to help myself to tell them in the classroom. During the last several years of my teaching career (35 years of high school science—physics, earth science, chemistry, biology) I was in the habit of using the final few minutes of each class to tell jokes and stories to my students. That time is usually wasted anyhow as students are thinking about leaving and going to their next class. After I began this practice, I found that they were actually looking forward to the jokes each day.

My problem was keeping track of the jokes I told. At first, I had each joke on a 3" by 5" card and would mark numbers on the cards, such as 3,4,5, etc. to indicate the class periods the jokes were told. But this became confusing.

So I decided to compile them into a book format. On each page I have included a variety of jokes, sayings, and stories. Sometimes I would simply read an entire page. Usually I started out with a longer joke or story and then used a bunch of one-liners. I decided to use the long joke first, because students would be paying better attention at the beginning of my reading.

As you will imagine, I despaired of attempts to organize the jokes into categories. Each time I read jokes, I wanted a variety.

After I retired from teaching, I began to think that perhaps other teachers could benefit from my work. Teachers are sometimes accused by their students and the public for being staid, stuffed-shirt types completely lacking a sense of humor. Nothing could be further from the truth.

Usually a teacher does not tell jokes because he simply has not had the time (or taken the time) to collect or organize

them or he may view them as a distraction. A teacher's "free time" is consumed with daily lesson planning, studying material he or she has forgotten, typing tests and quizzes, checking papers and entering the numbers and/or grades in the grade book and computer, calculating grade point averages, and recording them in both the grade book and computer. This is just a bare outline of his or her duties. Full time teaching is extremely time-consuming. Even selecting jokes takes extra time; I have already done this for the teacher.

By compiling jokes in this manner, I have endeavored to have enough to last a school year or about 180 days. A simple solution would be to have 180 pages and use a page each day. In actual practice, I found that I was not always using the entire page each day. To keep track for each class, I jotted down (in my plan book) the number of the last joke I told in that class. Nobody likes to be told the same joke twice.

The jokes in the first part of this book (pp.1-180) are all fairly clean and acceptable for use in the classroom. After I retired, I kept collecting jokes, and the jokes became somewhat "raunchier." However, most of them can be used by most teachers in high school classrooms.

Naturally, I tried to censor them, but it was not always successful. Early in the year I explained that I would not use ethnic, racial, or gross sexual jokes. Many of the ethnic jokes can be turned into moron-type jokes which is what I did and encouraged them to do.

ACKNOWLEDGEMENTS

Students would often ask me, "Where do you get all these jokes?" My answer was, "Everywhere." Most of them are in the public domain. They have been told over and over again. The original source is often not known. Many have been given to me by students over the years; they seemed to like the gross jokes or off-color jokes so they could see my face turn red.

Other sources of these jokes include the funny paper or comics in daily newspapers, old joke books, members of my family and relatives, neighbors, friends, and radio and TV talk shows.

In fact, I'd like to credit some of my inspiration to two men—Tom Healy and Del Donahoo who told "terrible" jokes on their early morning TV news program on Channel 3, Cleveland. It ran from 6:30 a.m. until 7:00 a.m. (in the 1980s) while I was eating breakfast, before walking to school. I enjoyed these terrible jokes, words of dubious wisdom, and the hammy performances of these two men. Tom Healy was always teasing Del Donahoo. Even today, long after these good jokers have died, I recall some of their jokes which made their way into my book and made me LOL (laugh out loud). Their jokes, laughter, and antics put me in a good mood for the day.

Another person to whom I need to give credit, was A.A. Silvidi, PhD, a professor of physics at Kent State University. He told at least one joke or story at the end of each physics class. I found myself looking forward to them. "Well," I'd say to myself, "what is the old codger going to tell us today?" The jokes and stories served as comic relief for the serious subject matter we were studying. After all, physics (as well as all of the sciences) can be very cut and dried subjects,. The little jokes and stories humanize the teacher and make the students realize that the teacher might be just like Dad, Mom, or anybody else.

The students to whom I read these jokes and stories were all Juniors and Seniors in high school, their ages between 16 and 18, enrolled in my physics and chemistry classes. Nearly all of them appreciated hearing the jokes and stories.

Some critics—teachers, administrators, parents, even some students— might say that the jokes and stories are irrelevant and a waste of time. I agree that they are irrelevant, but they are not a waste of time.

Educators will ask: What is the educational value of these jokes and stories? Here is my answer: They require students to listen carefully so they can understand the punch line, if there is one. They may even encourage students to ask questions to clarify some things they don't understand.

Why does scientific subject matter have to be crammed into the last few minutes? Students enjoy a break from difficult subject matter, and so does the teacher.

By using this joke book, teachers will have a supply of jokes and stories for each of the 180 school days of the year. Of course, I cannot dictate to the teacher and tell him or her what to do. They have to make up their minds about the use of humor (in the last few minutes) to lighten the educational load and help to make the classroom a fun place to be. At least, they might give this plan a try. As the epitaph on a tombstone read: "It's later than you think. Live, love, and loaf a little."

I should like to extend my personal thanks to Mr. and Mrs. Arthur Ramirez (Art and Linda) for their editing and proofreading It goes without saying, but I'll say it anyhow: Thanks, Art and Linda, for your love, friendship, and encouragement.

4

Thanks for reading the preface. HERE ARE THE JOKES and STORIES:

1. A man walked into a bar and ordered a beer. He had to leave to make a phone call, but he did not want anyone at the bar to swipe his beer, so he printed on a napkin next to the bottle of beer:

   WORLD's GREATEST KAROTE CHAMPION

   When he came back, the bottle of beer was empty.

   The napkin was turned over and printed on it were these Words:

   WORLD's FASTEST RUNNER

2. A man went to see his doctor. The doctor said to him, "Come on over to the window and stick out your tongue."

   The man was puzzled, but he went over to the window and stuck out his tongue. Then he said to the doctor, "Is the light better over here?"

   "No," the doctor replied, "I'm mad at my neighbor."

3. The Sunday school teacher asked her class, "Who led the children of Israel across the Red Sea?"

   No one knew.

   She picked out a new boy and asked him.

   The new boy said, "It wasn't me. We just moved here from Missouri."

4. Q. Why should you save your burned out light bulbs?

   A. So you can use them in your dark room.

5. Q. Did you hear what happened to the cow that jumped over the moon?

   A. It was an udder (utter) disaster?

6. A mother said to her child's teacher, "My youngest boy is troubled with halitosis."

   The teacher said, "Too bad. How did he get it?"

   The mother replied, "He hasn't got it. He just can't spell it."

7. Q. Think about Noah's ark. Which animal carried the most with him on the ark? And which animal carried the least?

   A. The elephant brought a trunk and the rooster only a comb.

8. After a round of partying, the man said to his girlfriend, "Do you tell your mother everything you do when you go out on a date?"

   The girl replied, "No, she doesn't care. It's my husband who wants to know everything."

9. A man was riding down an old dusty road in his horse pulled buggy. His dog was riding next to him on the seat. The man struck the horse with his whip, yelling "Go faster."

   The horse stopped, turned around and said, "Hey, don't hit me."

   Then the man said, "I didn't know that horses could talk."

   The dog looked up and said, "Oh, neither did I."

10. Q. What question can you never answer YES to?

    A. Are you asleep?

11. Q. What animal has the highest level of intelligence?

    A. Giraffe

12. Q. Why did the moron put his bed in the fireplace?

    A. Because he wanted to sleep like a log.

13. A woman's husband was missing. She went to the police station to make a report.

    An officer asked her, "Can you describe your husband?"

She said, "He's five feet tall. He weighs 98 pounds. He's bald headed. He wears false teeth. He chews tobacco and the juice is always running down his chin…On second thought, Officer, Just forget the whole thing." She turned and walked out of the police station.

14. A lady patient said to her doctor, "Doctor, do you think the scar on my stomach will show?"

   The doctor replied, "Well, madam, that's entirely up to you."

15. The minister said, "It will be nice and peaceful up there in heaven. There will be no buying and selling."

   One of the businessmen in the congregation stood up and said, "That's right. Because that is not where business has gone."

16. Son: "Pop, I got into trouble at school today and it's all your fault."

   Pop: "How's that?"

   Son: "Remember I asked you how much $500,000 was."

   Pop: "Yes, I remember."

   Son: "Well, you told me the wrong answer. 'A hell of a lot' ain't the right answer."

17. Q. What would happen if Bat Man and Robin were run over by a ruck? What would you call them?

   A. Flat Man and Ribbon.

18. Student: "Teacher, I don't think I deserved a zero on that test."

   Teacher: "I don't think so either, but that is the lowest mark I am allowed to give."

19. Q. What is the difference between an old dime and a new penny?

   A. Nine cents

20. She: "Now that we are engaged, dear, you'll give me a ring, won't you?"

    He: "Certainly. What's your number, darling?"

21. A moron asked the librarian, "Can you tell me a good book to read?"

    The librarian, somewhat confused, said, "Do you want something light or do you prefer a heavier book?

    The moron replied, "It really don't make no difference. You see, I have my pick-up truck parked right outside."

22. Two small boys were talking together. One said, "My father is a doctor. I can be sick for nothing."

    The other boy said, "My father is a preacher. I can be **good** for nothing."

23. The preacher asked a group of young boys, "Is there a devil?"

    One boy replied, "Naw, it's like Santa Claus. It's my daddy."

24. A father said to his son, "I'd rather you'd fail in school than cheat."

    His son said, "If that's what you want, I guarantee results."

25. Farmer: "Did you hear about the bee that flew in the cow's ear?"

    Friend: "No, what happened to him?"

    Farmer: "The bee wound up in a pail of milk."

    Friend: "How'd he do that?"

    Farmer: "He went in one ear and out the udder" (other)

26. A chemistry professor wrote a formula on the blackboard. He then called on a student, "Mr. Jones, what does HCl mean?"

    Student: "Well, oh, ah, I've got it right on the tip of my tongue, sir."

Chemistry professor: "Well, you'd better spit it out. It's hydrochloric acid."

27. Riddle: What is the longest word in the English language?

    Answer: SMILES

    Why? Because there is a mile between the first and last letter.

28. A man said to his girlfriend, "Will you marry me and spend the rest of your life with me?"

    Girlfriend: "No."

    The man said, "How about weekends?"

29. Q. What do you get when cross a dog with a chicken?

    A. Pooched eggs.

30. A man wanted to buy a dog. He went into a pet store. The pet store owner was trying to sell him a big black dog. He said, "This dog is well trained. You can give him money and he'll go to the store and bring back a newspaper for you."

    So the man bought the dog. An hour later the man returned to the pet store. He said, "I gave the dog some money, but he has not returned with the paper. And it's been more than an hour."

    The pet store owner asked, "How much money did you give him?"

    The man said, "Five dollars."

    The pet store owner said, "Oh, when you give him five dollars, he goes to the movies."

31. A doctor said to his patient, "Why haven't you been following my directions and taking your medicine?"

    The patient said, "I have been, Doctor. The label on the bottle says, 'Keep the bottle tightly closed at all times.'"

32. Sunday school teacher: "Now, Charlie, who was Goliath?"

    Charlie: "Goliath was the man David rocked to sleep."

33. Passenger on an ocean-going ship: "Say, Captain, I'm sick. How far are we from land?"

    Captain: "About three miles."

    Passenger: "Which way?"

    Captain: "Straight down."

34. The Coast Guard received a mayday message: "Help! We're in the water!"

    The radio operator asked, "Capsize?"

    After a long silence, the voice answered, "Six and seven-eights."

35. On the first day of school, a young woman teacher wrote on the blackboard, "I ain't had no fun all summer." Then she turned around and pointed to a teen age boy and said, "Now, Johnnie, what shall I do to correct this?"

    Johnny replied, "Get a boyfriend."

36. Riddle: What do they call Ex-Lax in Holland?

    Answer: Dutch Cleanser

37. It was the young married couple's first argument about money. She said, "Before we were married, you said you were well off."

    He said, "I was, but I didn't know it."

38. Q. What did the scientist get when he crossed a chicken with a silk worm?

    A. He got a hen that lays eggs with panty hose in them.

39. Q. What is the daffynition of DIPLOMACY?

    A. The ability to tell a man to go to hell so that he looks forward to the trip.

40.   A housewife called a refrigerator repair man. He fixed her refrigerator in one minute.

Housewife: "How much do I owe you?"

Repairman: "$50.00."

Housewife: "That's ridiculous. You only worked one minute."

Repairman: "$50.00."

Housewife: "I want an itemized statement."

So the repairman wrote on a piece of paper:

Turning a screw -- $2.00

Knowing which screw to turn—"$48.00.":

Total $50.00

41.   A mother took her son to see the doctor. The doctor asked, "What's wrong with him?"

The mother replied, "He swallowed a nickel. Then he coughed up three dimes. What should I do?"

The doctor laughed and said,"Keep feeding him nickels."

42.   A Sunday school teacher said, "Now, children, I have told you the story of Jonah and the Whale." She pointed to one of her students. "Willie, will you tell me what this story means?"

"Yes," said Willie. "It means that you can't keep a good man down."

43.   A customer in a restaurant was ready to order dessert. He asked the waitress, ""What flavors of ice cream do you have?"

The waitress, in a hoarse whisper, said "vanilla, chocolate, strawberry, mint….."

The customer said, "Do you have laryngitis?"

The waitress continued in a hoarse whisper, "No, just vanilla chocolate, strawberry, mint….."

44. A peddler on the city street walked up to a man and asked him, "Do you want to buy a watch?"

   The man looked at the peddler and he thought to himself—*It's probably stolen.* So he said, "Is it hot?"

   The peddler replied, "I don't know. I didn't take its temperature."

45. A law student stole a car and he was being tried in court. The Judge said, "Now, tell the court how you came to steal the car."

   The law student replied, "Well, sir, the car was parked in front of the cemetery. So naturally I thought the owner was dead." [Editor's note: This one will go over like a lead balloon. The law student must be a moron.]

46. Q. How is a graveyard like a bathroom?

   A. When you gotta go, you gotta go.

47. A man returned from his trip to foreign country. His friend asked him, "Did you learn any Spanish in Mexico?"

   The man replied, "No, but I picked up a little Cuban one night in Havana."

48. Q. Why did the scientist cross a turkey with a centipede

   A. So everyone could have a drumstick for Thanksgiving.

49. Q. What is the daffynition of an undertaker?

   A. The last man to let you down.

50. A man threw a quarter toward the blind man's cup. The coil missed and rolled along the sidewalk, but the man in the dark glasses quickly recovered it.

   The man who tossed the quarter said, "But I thought you were blind."

The man in the dark glasses said, "No, I'm not the regular blind man, sir. I'm just taking his place while he's at the movies."

51. A patient, sitting in the dental chair, said, "Hey, Doc, what should I do about my yellow teeth?"

    The dentist replied, "Wear a brown tie."

52. Two little girls were comparing notes in catechism study. One girl said, "I've got to original sin. How far have you got?"

    The other girl said, "Oh, I'm way beyond redemption."

53. A teenager was on the telephone for one half hour. After she hung up, her father asked her, "You usually are on the phone for two hours. What stopped you this time?"

    The girl replied, "Wrong number."

54. Q. What is the biggest jewel in the world?

    A. A baseball diamond.

55. Q. When is a door not a door?

    A. When it's a jar.

56. Two principals were discussing what they'd like to do after they retired. The first principal said, "I'd like to be superintendent of an orphans' home so I'd never get any telephone calls from parents."

    The second principal said, "I want to be a warden of a penitentiary. The alumni never come back to visit.."

57. Q. Do you know why an acrobat's life is like a girl's underwear?

    A. Because one slip is enough.

58. Did you hear about the girl who went to Ohio State and got her PhD in six months without cracking a book?

    How did she do that?

She married him?

59.   Q. What do you get when you cross a dummy with a flower?

A. A blooming idiot.

60.   Q. What is the daffynition of a WILL?

A. A dead giveaway.

61.   Knock knock

Who's there?

Sea shell.

Sea shell who?

She shall have music wherever she goes.

62.   Q. Why is the funeral business so profitable?

A. People are just dying to get in.

63.   An insurance salesman tried to sell a doctor a mal practice policy. The doctor was hard to sell.

So the insurance man said, "What if a man died as he was leaving the doctor's office?"

The doctor replied, "I'd turn him around and say he was coming in."

64.   Dennis the Menace went to church one Sunday morning with some of his friends. When he got home, his mother asked him, "Did you behave in church?"

Dennis replied, "Of course I did. I heard the lady back of us say she never saw a child <u>behave</u> so."

65.   A visitor at a casino in Las Vegas saw three men and a dog playing poker. The visitor said, "He must be a smart dog. Isn't he real smart?"

One of the employees said, "No. He's not smart."

The visitor said, "He must be smart. I never saw a dog play poker."

The employee said, "No, he's not smart. Every time he gets a good hand, he wags his tail."

66. Customer: "I want some nails."

    Clerk: "That will be $1.25 plus tax."

    Customer: I just want nails—no tacks. (TAX)

67. Moron wife says to her moron husband, "Our son's teacher says our son ought to have an encyclopedia."

    Her husband replied, "Let him walk to school like I did."

68. Q. If a carrot and a lettuce were racing, which one would win?

    A. The lettuce. Because it's a head (ahead)

69. Q. If an orange and a tomato have a race, who will win?

    A. The tomato. Because it can always catsup. (catchup)

70. A man had a wife named Kate. He started seeing his mistress named Edith. His wife found out about his mistress. What did she say to her husband? You can't have your Kate and Edith, too. (You can't have your cake and eat it, too.).

71. Q. What do you get when you cross an elephant with a rhinoceros?

    A. An ellarhino.

    Q. What is an ellarhino?

    A. Hell if I know.

72. Q. What is the daffynition of a drive in?

    A. That's a place where a man can turn off his ignition and try out his clutch.

73. Knock knock

Who's there?

Sara

Sara who?

Sara (Is there a) doctor in the house?

74. A man in western North Carolina got sick and went to a doctor. The doctor treated him for a month or so, and he seemed to get worse. Finally the doctor told him, "You need a change of climate. Why don't you go to Florida for the rest of the winter?" So the man moved to Florida. He lay out in the sun and got a good suntan, but in two weeks he died.

    They shipped his body home to North Carolina. At his funeral two of his old friends came by his casket to view him for the last time. He looked good with his suntan and his new suit. One friend said to the other, "Those two weeks in Florida sure did him a world of good."

75. A patient said to her doctor, "Doctor, I have terrible nightmares. Just as the alarm goes off, I escape from this horrible monster. What should I do?"

    The doctor replied, "Never forget to set the alarm."

76. A regular churchgoer noticed across the aisle a neighbor who boasted of being a confirmed atheist. As they walked out of the church, the regular churchgoer asked, "What are you doing in church? I thought you were a confirmed atheist."

    "I was, but I gave it up. Do you know why I gave it up?"

    "No. Why?"

    "No holidays," said the former atheist."

77. Two farmers went to Kentucky and bought hay at $5.00 a bale. Then they brought it to Ohio and sold it at the same price--$5.00 per bale.

    One farmer said, "We don't seem to be making any money."

The other farmer said, "Maybe we should get a bigger truck."

78.   Q. Did you ever hear about frozen bandages? Do you know what they are used for?

A. Cold cuts

79.   A teacher asked her class, "What is the difference between ignorance and apathy?" Nobody seemed to know. She called on Tommy, a recalcitrant boy who liked to make trouble. She said, "Tommy, what is the answer?"

Tommy shouted, "I don't know and I don't care."

The teacher said, "Tommy, that is the first correct answer you've given this year."

80.   Q. How can your pocket be empty and still have something in it?

A. When it has a hole.

81.   Q. Why should a husband hold his wife's hand in a movie theatre?

A. That's to keep her from eating all the popcorn.

82.   Q. What kind of fish like peanut butter?

A. Jelly fish

83.   Q. What is the daffynition of socialized medicine?

A. That's when women get together and talk about their doctors and operations.

84.   Knock, knock.

Who's there?

Gladys

Gladys who?

Glad it's Friday, how about you?

85. A man went into a doctor's office with two badly burned ears. "What happened to your ears?" the doctor asked.

"Well, I was ironing when the telephone rang. I accidentally reached for the iron instead of the telephone."

The doctor said, "I can understand why you had one ear burned, but how did you get both ears burned."

The man said, "The telephone rang again."

86. A little boy said to his rich grandfather, "Grandpa, can you make a sound like a frog?"

The grandfather said, "Why should I do that?"

The little boy replied, "Because Daddy says that when you croak we'll all be rich."

87. There was a convention going on, and the main speaker was sitting in a chair behind the podium. He suddenly remembered that he had forgotten his dentures; they were back in the hotel room. He nudged the fellow sitting beside him and said, "I've got to go back in my hotel room and get my dentures."

The fellow he nudged, a fellow speaker, said, "You don't have enough time." He reached into his pocket and pulled out a pair of dentures. He said, "Here, try these."

The main speaker tried them and said, "No. They won't work."

The other speaker said, "Well, wait a minute." He then reached into another pocket and pulled out another set of dentures.

The main speaker tried them and said, "Hey, they work pretty good. I believe I can use them."

After he made his speech, he took the dentures out of his mouth and returned them. He said to the good Samaratan, "Gee, thanks. I was lucky to be sitting next to a dentist."

The man said, "Dentist! Hell No, I'm an undertaker!"

88.   Q. When does a bed change size?

        A. At night when two feet are added.

89.   Patient: If you think you are losing your memory, what should you do?

        Psychiatrist: Forget it.

90.   Q. Do you want to see a model home?

        A. Sure do. When does she get off work?

91.   Joe: "She's a lady carpenter."

        Moe: "What's so great about that?"

        Joe: "You ought to see her build."

92.   Q. What do you call a rabbit with a lot of fleas?

        A. Bugs Bunny

93.   The cynic says, "A man with a clear conscience has a bad mmory."

94.   Knock, knock

        Who's there?

        Your Avon lady and your door bell is broken.

95.   Q. Kleptomania is a disease. If you have kleptomania, what can you do about it?

        A. You can take something for it.

96.   Teacher: "Use the word AMAZON in a sentence."

        Student: "You can pay for the eggs, but the amazon me." (ham is on)

97.   A lady patient said to her doctor, "Doctor, I'm having terrible nightmares."

        The doctor said, "Describe them to me."

"Well, last night I dreamed I was a wigwam. And the night before I dreamed I was a teepee. What's wrong with me?"

The doctor said, "You're two tents." (too tense)

98. The Sunday school teacher was collecting money as she usually did from her pupils. One little boy held onto his dollar bill and did not put it in the bowl.

She said to him, "Don't you want to donate your dollar for Christian missionary work?"

The little boy said, "'I'd rather go down to the drug store and buy a chocolate soda."

The Sunday school teacher then said, "Don't you want to contribute your dollar to a good cause?"

The little boy said, "I'd rather get the chocolate soda and then the druggist can give the dollar for a good cause."

99. Son: "If men go to heaven, why don't angels have whiskers?"

Father: "Because men get to heaven by a very close shave."

100. Q. Did you ever have any acting experience?

A. Sure, my leg was once in a cast.

101. Q. What is the daffynition of ignorance?

A. It's when you don't know something and somebody else (like the teacher) finds it out.

102. Q. If F O L K spells folk, how do you spell the white of an egg?

A. The narrator waits for the person to say Y O L K. Then the narrator says, "Wrong" and spells it: "W H I T E"

103. Q. What do you do when in doubt about kissing a girl?

A. Give her the benefit of the doubt.

104. Q. What do you get when you cross a snake with a rabbit?

A. You get an adder that multiplies.

105.   Q. What is the daffynition of a taxpayer?

A. A citizen who does not have to take an examination to work for the government.

106.   Knock, knock

Who's there?

Sid.

Sid who?

Sid down. You're rocking the boat.

107.   Professor Williams, an expert on zoological nomenclature, was leading an expedition into the wilds of the upper Nile in Africa. One day an underling ran to him in a state of great excitement.

"Professor Williams," he cried, "Something dreadful has just happened. Your wife has been swallowed by an alligator."

A deep look of concern came over Williams' face. "Surely, Jackson," he said, "You mean a crocodile."

108.   A patient said to his dentist, "How come you are charging me three times as much as other patients?"

The dentist said, "I had to. You yelled so loud you scared away two other patients."

109.   One little boy said to another little boy, "Why don't you come to my church?"

The other little boy said, "Because I belong to another abomination."

110.   You know the famous picture of Whistler's mother. She is sitting in a rocking chair. Once Whistler saw his mother, down on her hands and knees, scrubbing the floor. What did Whistler say to his mother when he saw her scrubbing the floor?

Answer: "Hey, Mom, you're off your rocker."

111.   Q. Did you hear about the 95 year old man who has AIDS? A. One in each year –hearing aids.

112.   Teacher: What does unaware mean?

Student: It's the last thing you take off at night and the first thing you put on in the morning.

113.   Q. What is the quietest game in the world?

A. Bowling. Why? You can hear a pin drop.

114.   Q. What is a cat's favorite dessert?

A. Mice cream.

115.   Q. Which moves faster—heat or cold?

A. Heat. Why: Because you can catch cold.

116.   A man said to his friend, "You say you are going to marry a woman with one million dollars a year income, and you say it's a love match!"

His friend said, "Certainly, it's a love match. I love money."

117.   First Moron: "I got me one of those suits with two pairs of pants."

Second Moron: "How do you like it?"

First Moron: "Not so well. "It's too hot wearing two pairs of pants."

118.   Q. What is the daffynition of a spinster?

A. A woman who is unhappily unmarried.

119.   Q. What happened to the two bedbugs who fell in love?

A. They got married in the spring.

120.   A man was arrested for stealing. The Judge asked him, "Where were you stealing?"

He replied, "Oh, here and there."

The Judge asked, "When were you stealing?"

He replied, "Oh, now and then."

The Judge said to the police officer, "Lock him up."

He asked, "When do I get out?"

The Judge replied, "Sooner or later."

121. Doctor: "Don't worry. You are going to make a complete recovery."

Patient: "But, how can you be so sure, doctor? I thought this was a very serious disease with a petty poor outlook."

Doctor: "It is. The textbooks say nine out of ten patients with your condition die."

Patient: "Well then, how can you be so optimistic in my case?"

Doctor: "Just a matter of statistics. You are the tenth case I've treated, and the other nine are already dead."

122. A man had been a loafer all his life. His wife was always trying to get him to help with jobs around the house, but he always refused. His wife did all the work. When he died she had his body cremated and she put the ashes in an hour glass. She put the hour glass on the mantle above the fireplace. Underneath she printed a sign. What did It say?

AT WORK AT LAST

123. The guest speaker said, "I know this great joke about amnesia. If only could remember the punch line."

124. Customer: "How much are these tomatoes?"

Clerk: "One dollar a pound."

Customer: "Did you <u>raise</u> them yourself?"

Clerk: "I certainly did. They were only fifty cents a pound yesterday."

125. A mother's note to her daughter's teacher: "Please excuse Mary. She was sick and I had her shot."

126. Another blooper: "Ralph was absent because he was playing football and got hurt in the growing part." (groin)

127. The teacher said, "Johnnie, please use the word <u>bulletin</u> in a sentence."

    Johnnie said, "Dad got in a fight and now he has a <u>bulletin</u> in his leg." (bullet in)

128. Silly, silly. Q. What do Eskimos call their cows?

    A. Eskimoos..

129. Q. Why do Eskimos wash their clothes in Tide? (baby talk for inside)

    A. Because it's too cold to wash them outside?

130. Q. What animal goes to bed with its shoes on?

    A. a horse

131. Lawyer: "You mean you want to get a divorce on grounds of your husband's appearance?"

    Wife: "Yes. He hasn't shown up for five years."

132. Q: "Before you mailed that package, did you mark it FRAGILE and THIS END UP?"

    A: "I sure did. And to be extra safe, I marked it that way on both ends."

133. Q: What is the daffynition of dieting?

    A. The triumph of mind over platter.

134. A student was taking a true-false test. He was flipping a coil for each question. The teacher asked him, "Why are you flipping a coin?"

The student replied, "If it comes up heads, it's true. If it's tails, it's false.

Well, strangely enough, the smiling teacher did not say anything and went back to checking papers. Later on, near the end of the period, the same student was doing the same thing again. The teacher went back to the student's desk and asked him, "Why are you flipping the coin again?"

"I'm double checking my answers."

135. A woman said to her doctor, "My husband is at death's door."

The doctor handed her a bottle and said, "Have him take a bottle of this elixir. I' m sure it will pull him through."

136. A preacher went to see a woman whose husband had died. He asked her, "Was your husband covered by insurance when he died?"

She answered, "Oh, no, just his night shirt."

137. A son was in the driver's seat and learning to drive. His father was in the passenger's seat.

The son said, "Dad, what should I do if the brakes give way?"

His father said, "Hang onto the wheel and head for something cheap."

138. Q. Who were the first gamblers?

A. Adam and Eve.

Q. Why were Adam and Eve the first gamblers?

A. Didn't they shake a paradise? (pair of dice)

139. A teacher teaching arithmetic said, "What is the difference between one yard and two yards?"

Johnnie raised his hand and said, "A fence."

140.　Q. How did McDonald celebrate his engagement to Wendy's?

　　　A. With an onion ring.

141.　Q. Why did the turtle cross the road?

　　　A. To get the Shell station.

142.　Q. Why did the potato cross the road?

　　　A. He saw a fork up ahead.

143.　The following is the romantic's poem:

　　　Tell me why the stars do shine;

　　　Tell me why the ivy twines.

　　　Tell me why the skies are blue.

　　　And I will tell you why I love you.

144.　The following is the answer of a scientist, imbued with a rationalistic view of the universe:

　　　Nuclear fusion makes stars to shine.

　　　Tropisms make the ivy twine.

　　　Rayleigh scattering makes skies so blue.

　　　Testicular hormones are why I love you.

145.　A Sunday school teacher asked her class about the part of the prayer that says, "Give us this day our daily bread…" She said, "Why in your prayers do you only ask for your daily bread instead of asking enough for a week?"

　　　Tommy raised his hand and answered, "So. we can get it fresh every day."

146.　Q. What is the daffynition of bacteria?

　　　A. Back door of a cafeteria.

147.   Knock, knock

Who's there?

Tarzan

Tarzan who?

Tarzan tripes forever. (stars and stripes forever)

148.   A man who'd lost his job went to an employment office. When the clerk asked him what he did for a living, he said, "Diesel fitter."

The clerk looked in her card file and said "Diesel fitter. That's a very skilled position. You're going to get $600 a month unemployment compensation."

A bit later, another unemployed man came into the office and the clerk asked him what he did for a living.

"I'm a crotch sewer," he replied.

"A crotch sewer?" the clerk said.

"Yeah," he said. "I work in a pantyhose factory. I take the right leg of the pantyhose and the left leg of the pantyhose and I sew in the crotch."

The clerk; went to her file and, lo and behold, found the occupation "crotch sewer."

"You know, that's not a very skilled position," she told him. "You're only going to get $100 a month unemployment compensation."

"One hundred a month!" the man exclaimed, "My friend was in here just a little while ago and you gave him $600 a month."

"But your friend is a diesel fitter," the clerk said, "and you are only a crotch sewer."

"Lady, he works right next to me on the pantyhose assembly line. I told you I take the right leg of the pantyhose and the left leg of the pantyhose and sew in the crotch. Then I hand the pantyhose to this guy, and he pulls the pantyhose over his head and yells, "Dese'll fit 'er."

149. A woman went to see her doctor. The doctor asked, "What's wrong?"

"Oh, Doctor, I don't know whether I've got amnesia, or is it magnesia? I don't know where I/m going."

The doctor said, "Lady, if you had magnesia, <u>you'd know</u> where you were going."

150. A new preacher, attempting to increase the membership in his country church, drove out in the country. He saw a farmer plowing a field. He pulled his car to the side of the road and started a conversation with the farmer. Soon, he said to the farmer, "Do you belong to the Christian family?"

The farmer said, "No, they live two farms down."

The preacher said, "No, no. I mean, Are you lost?"

The farmer said, "No, I've lived here thirty years."

The preacher: "I mean, Are you ready for Judgment Day?"

Farmer: "When is it?"

Preacher: "It could be today or tomorrow."

Farmer: "Well, when you find out for sure when it is, you let me know. My wife will probably want to go both days."

151. Q. Why does he ocean roar?

A. If you had crabs on your bottom, you'd roar, too.

152. Q. What did the toothless termite say when he walked into the saloon?

A. Where is the bar tender? Is the bar tender here?

153. Chemistry teacher: "What is the formula for water?"

Student: "H I J K L M N O."

Teacher: "Whoever told you that?"

Student: "You did. You said it was H to O."

154. Q. What did the ham say to the scrambled eggs?

A. What a crazy mixed up bunch of kids!

155. A man while watching a football game on TV fell asleep on the couch. His wife let him sleep there all night. Then, in the morning, she woke him up by saying, "Honey, it's twenty to seven."

He answered, "Whose favor?"

156. A commencement speaker at the Yale University graduation exercises was a gentleman with a powerful voice and remarkable wind.

He said, "There isn't a letter in YALE that does not tell its tale of wonderment and glory. Y, for instance, stands for YOUTH…" and for half an hour he told all the joys of youth, in tones of ecstasy.

With scarcely a pause for breath, he went on. "A is for AMBITION, and when I think of ambition joined with youth, words fail me…" except they did not for another half hour of strenuous exposition.

It was when he was well into the third half hour speech, devoting it to L for LABOR, that one writhing graduate whispered to his neighbor, "Thank God, this isn't the MASSACHUSETTS INSTITUTE OF TECHNOLOGY."

157. John: "I went to the dentist this morning."

Tom: "Does your tooth still hurt?"

John: "I don't know. The dentist kept it."

158. Sunday school teacher: "Where is God?"

Johnny raises his hand, "I know, teacher."

Sunday school teacher: "All right, Johnny, where is God?

Johnny: "God's in the bathroom."

Sunday school teacher: "Where did you get that idea?"

Johnny: "Well, when I was in the bathroom, Dad knocked on the door and yelled, "Lord, are you still in there?"

159. A woman went to a cemetery in San Francisco and put flowers on a grave. While she was doing this, she saw a Chinaman kneel and put a bowl of rice on a grave.

   She said to the Chinaman, "When will your friend come up and eat that rice?"

   The Chinaman replied, "The same time that your friend comes up to smell the flowers."

160. 1st man: "Isn't this beastly weather we're having?"

   2nd man: "I don't understand."

   1st man: "Isn't it raining cats and dogs?

161. Teacher: "What is a comet?"

   Student: "A star with a tail."

   Teacher: "Can you give me an example?"

   Student: "Lassie."

162. Q. Why did the moron put on a wet shirt?

   A. Because the label says WASH AND WEAR.

163. Q. Did you hear about the man with 16 wives?

   A. 4 – better. 4—worse, 4—richer, 4—poorer

164. Two young men were standing at a street corner. They were looking for dates. A pretty girl walked by, winked at one of

the men, and dropped her handkerchief. The man she winked at did not pick up the handkerchief and did not follow her.

The other man said, "You stupid idiot! Why didn't you pick up the handkerchief and follow her? She was asking to be picked up. Well, answer me."

The man replied, "I use Kleenex."

Seething with anger, the other man threw up his arms.

165. Q. Why did the moron wear his hair so long?

A. So that he could create the impression that his mind was fertile.

166. Q. What do you call a man who sells mobile homes?

A. A wheel estate dealer.

167. Two Englishmen, called Derrick and Quincy, met for dinner at the Lions Corner House in London.

Quincy: "I say, Derrick, how are you, old chap?"

Derrick: "Fine. Just fine. Lots doing. Business good. Children fine. Weather pleasant and all that sort of balderdash."

Quincy: "Jolly good. Anything else?"

Derrick: "Oh, yes, I buried my wife."

Quincy: "Really!"

Derrick: "Had to. Dead, you know."

168. Nurse: "How is the man who swallowed the spoon?"

Doctor: "He can hardly stir."

169. A man said to his friend, "My doctor said he'd have me on my feet in two weeks."

"And did he?" his friend asked.

"He sure did. To pay his bill, I had to sell my car. Now I'm walking everywhere."

170.   Q. When is it hard to; drive a bargain?

A. When you have to drive a second hand car.

171.   A preacher said to a man drinking whiskey, "Don't you know that stuff is slow poison?"

The man drinking whiskey replied, "That's O.K. I ain't in no hurry."

172.   A barber was shaving a one arm man. The barber asked him, "Have I shaved you before?"

The one arm man replied, "No. I lost my arm in a saw mill accident."

173.   A man got a job at a zoo. His job was to take care of the bears. When a bear got out of hand, he had to use a noose and drop it over the bear's head and pull the bear out of the cage. He finally quit this job.

A friend asked him, "Why did you quit that job?"

He replied, "I just don't want to be the nooser of bad bears anymore." (Translation: I don't want to be the bearer of bad news any more.)

174.   A young man wearing a parachute is about to jump out of an airplane. He says to his instructor standing next to him, "What if the parachute does not open?"

The instructor replies, "That is known as what is called JUMPING TO CONCLUSIONS."

175.   Student: "How does science help business?"

Teacher: "What would the suspender business amount to without the Law of Gravitation?"

176.   Q. Why did the farmer put bells on his cow?

A. The cow's horns didn't work.

177. Q. Why is it wise to bring a watch into the desert?

    A. Because every watch has a spring.

178. Q. How do you know a river is rich?

    A. Because it has two banks.

179. Q. When is a boat affectionate?

    A. When it hugs the shore.

180. First football widow: "How do you get your husband to come to bed?"

    Second football widow: "I have a night gown made of astro turf."

181. Q. What do you get when you cross poison ivy with a shamrock (4 leaf clover)?

    A. A rash of good luck.

182. A man went into a hotel. He said to the room clerk, "I have a reservation."

    Clerk: "What is your name?"

    Man: "John Smith."

    Clerk: "No. I don't have a reservation for you," he said after looking in the file.

    Man: "I made a reservation."

    Clerk: "We're completely filled."

    Man: "What if President Obama showed up tonight? Would you have a room for him?"

    Clerk: "Oh, yes." (somewhat flustered)

    Man: "Well, President Obama is not coming tonight. I'll take his room."

183. A husband was going over bills. He became very irate when he saw a doctor bill for his wife. He said, "Do you mean that you gave that doctor $80 and all he did was pain your throat!"

    His wife said calmly, ""What did you expect? Wallpaper?

184. After applying the stethoscope, the doctor said "I don't like the sound of your heart. You have had some trouble with angina pectoris, haven't you?"

    "You're right in a way, Doctor," said the young man sheepishly, "Only that isn't her name."

185. A wife said to her friend, "We dined royally last night."

    Her friend said, "What do you mean?"

    The wife replied, "First my husband took me to Burger King. Then, for dessert, he took me to Dairy Queen."

186. Q. Why are oysters lazy?

    A. Because they are always found in beds?

    Q. Why are fish smart?

    A. Because they swim in schools

187. English teacher: "Tommy, please tell me what it is when I say: I love. You love. He loves."

    Tommy: "That's one of them love triangles where somebody gets shot."

188. Q. Why does an elephant have a trunk?

    A. Because he does not have a glove compartment.

189. Q. Why did the grandmother put roller skates on her rocking chair?

    A. Because she wanted to rock and roll.

190. Q. A man drove for twenty years and never had a complaint from a backseat driver. Why?

A. Because he drove a hearse.

191.   A woman's first husband died. Within a year she was married again. After a few weeks she was seen in the grocery store wearing all black clothes.

An acquaintance asked her, "Why are you wearing black? Did you second husband die, too?"

"No, but lately he has become so impossible that I went into mourning for my first husband."

192.   Q. Why did the moron throw the clock out the window?

A. Because he wanted to see time fly.

193.   Mr. Flea said to Mr. Flea, "Mrs. Flea, why do you look so sad?"

Mrs. Flea replied, "My children are all going to the dogs."

194.   This happened in Las Vegas. A man went over to another man on the sidewalk in front of a casino and said, "Can you lend me one hundred dollars?"

The second man said, "Why should I lend you one hundred dollars?"

The first man said, "My wife and kids are in our hotel room, and they are starving."

The second man said, "How do I know you're not going to take this money and gamble with it and probably lose it?"

The first man said, "Oh, gambling money, I've got."

195.   Patient: "Doctor, I want to thank you for your great medicine."

Doctor: "It helped you, did it?"

Patient: "It helped me wonderfully."

Doctor: "How many bottles did you find it necessary to take?"

Patient: "Oh, I didn't take any of it. My uncle took one bottle and I am his sole heir."

196. Two students were comparing notes before taking an English literature exam. The first student said, "Great Scott! I've forgotten who wrote *Ivanhoe*."

     The second student said, "I'll tell you if you tell me who in the dickens wrote *The Tale of Two Cities*."

197. A lady bought a parrot at a pet shop. She returned the next day and said to the clerk, "That parrot I bought yesterday uses terrible language."

     "That's O.K.," the clerk said, "You should be glad he also does not drink or gamble."

198. Q. What time of day was Adam born?

     A. Just before Eve.

199. Q. What is worse than raining cats and dogs?

     A. Hailing taxi cabs.

200. A boy said to his father, "I answered a question in class today."

     His father said, "What was the question?"

     The boy said, "Who broke the window?"

201. Q. What is the difference between a jeweler and a jailer?

     A. A jeweler sells watches, and a jailer watches cells.

202. Q. When is a face not a face?

     A. When it becomes a little pale. (pail)

203. Q. Why is an icy sidewalk like music?

     A. Because if you do not See sharp, you will Be flat.

204. A wife said to her husband "Where have you been so long?"

     Her husband replied, "I was talking to myself and I couldn't get away."

205. Eve said to Adam, "You know, Adam, you should really try to take more pride in your appearance."

    Adam replied, "Strange you should say that, Eve, because I've been thinking about turning over a new leaf."

206. Did you hear about the strip-tease artist who arrived in Hollywood with ten empty suitcases?

207. Knock, knock

    Who's there?

    Augusta

    Augusta who?

    A gust of wind.

208. Christmas is the season when your neighbor's radio keeps you awake all night playing "Silent Night."

209. What do you do in December – Jingle bells.

    What do you do in January –Juggle bills.

210. Q. Why does a cat on a beach remind you of Christmas?

    A. Sandy claws. (Santa Claus)

211. Q. Why does Santa Claus like to work in his garden?A. Because he likes to Ho! Ho! Ho!

212. Q. Which of Santa's reindeer is light on his feet?

    A. Dancer

213. Q. Do you know that one of Santa's reindeer is missing this year?

    A. It's Comet.

    Q. Why is Comet missing?

    A. Santa left him at home to clean the sink.

214. Q. What did Adam say to Eve on the day before Christmas?

A. It's Christmas, Eve.

215.   Mrs. Claus heard a noise on the roof. She said to Santa Claus, "What is that noise on the roof?"

Santa replied, ""It's rain, dear." (reindeer)

216.   Q. What are the four stages of man?

A. First, I believed in Santa Claus.

Second, I didn't believe in Santa Claus.

Third, Now I am Santa Claus.

Fourth, Now I also look like Santa Claus.

217.   Q. Did you hear about the penny pinching honeymoon couple who wanted to go to Niagara Falls but did not want to spend the money. Do you know what they did instead?

A. They stayed home and listened to the roar of Niagara Falls on their tape recorder.

218.   Q. What do doctors and storks have in common?

A. Big bills.

219.   Q. Did you ever see the Catskill Mountains?

A. No, but I've seen them kill mice.

220.   A student took his report card home at the end of the semester, in January. His mother looked at it and said, "What's the trouble? Why do you have so many poor grades—Ds and Fs—this month?"

Her son replied, "Mom, there's no trouble. You know yourself that things are always marked down after the holidays."

221.   Q. Why aren't there any alligators left in Florida?

A. Because they all have Gator Aids.

222.   Q. What is the daffynition of an octopus?

A. An eight legged cat. (pus for pussy or cat)

223.   Q. What do you get when you mix Milk of Magnesia with Holy Water?

    A. A religious movement.

224.   The following story was told to me by my cousin, Sally Hopkins, in Colorado:

    Two young Indian braves were named Falling Rock and Straight Arrow. The time came when they had to go out in the woods and prove that they were men. They did these things and Straight Arrow came back to make a report to his Chief.

    Straight Arrow said, "Look at what I've done. I've killed a buffalo and made a buffalo robe to keep my body warm at night. I've killed a deer and made moccasins and clothes for myself."

    The Chief said, ""O.K., you pass. You've proven that you are a real man. But what about Falling Rock? Where is he?"

    Straight Arrow said, "He was following me, but I don't know what happened to him."

    The Chief told him, "Go out and look for him."

    Straight Arrow went out to look for Falling Rock, but he could not find him. The Chief then sent out other young braves to look for Falling Rock, but nobody could find him. Finally the Chief put up a sign: WATCH OUT FOR FALLING ROCK. And the sign has been there ever since.

225.   A man was admitted to the hospital. He had AIDS, herpes, and syphilis. He was put in a room all by himself. He was then put on a diet of pepperoni pizza and pancakes.

    Q. Why did they put him on a diet of pepperoni pizza and pancakes?

A. That's the only kind of thing they could slide under the door.

226.   Q. Why is it that they always give a shower for a prospective bride but never for a prospective bridegroom?

A. He doesn't need one. He's all washed up, anyhow.

227.   Little girl: "Daddy, what color are fleas?"

Daddy: "Black."

Little girl: "I don't think so."

Daddy: "Why not?"

Little girl: "Remember: 'Mary had a little lamb whose <u>fleas</u> (fleece) was white as snow.'"

228.   Farmer: "Do you have a water melon patch?"

City slicker: "Why, is the melon leaking?"

229.   It's as exciting as watching grass grow or paint dry.

230.   He's such a good talker he could talk a dog off a meat truck.

231.   Teacher: She writes on the blackboard: I HAVE WENT. Then she turns to the class and says, "That's wrong, isn't it?"

Johnny says, "Yes, ma'am."

Teacher: "Why is it wrong, Johnny?"

Johnny: "Because you ain't went yet."

232.   Q. What is another name for a grandfather clock?

A. An old timer.

233.   Q. What do you call a cow lying on the ground?

A. Ground beef.

234.   Q. What am I? I speak every language, but I never went to school.

A. An echo

235.　What are the three essentials for sex education?

KNOWLEDGE -- Knowing what to do.

SKILL – Knowing how to do it.

WISDOM – Not doing it.

236.　Two men and a moron were driving across the country when their car broke down. They asked a nearby farmer if they could sleep in his barn. The farmer grudgingly agreed, but said, "You had better be quiet, though, I don't like prowlers, and I'm likely to shoot first and ask questions later."

The three men agreed not to make any noise and lay down to sleep, but eventually one of them had to get up to go to the bathroom. As he stumbled down the stairs in the dark, he heard the farmer cock his rifle and shout, "Who's there?"

"MEOW," said the man, and the farmer went back to bed.

A little while later, the second man, too, felt the call of nature. He stumbled down the stairs in the dark. The farmer shouted, "Who's there?"

The man said, "MEOW," and the jumpy farmer was quieted and went back to bed.

When it was the moron's turn to go to the bathroom, he got down as far as the foot of the stairs before the farmer shouted, "Who in the hell is that?"

The moron replied, "It's me, the cat."

237.　Patient: "Doctor, do you think I shall live until I'm 90?"

Doctor: "How old are you?"

Patient: "Forty."

Doctor: "Do you drink, gamble, smoke, or haves any vices of any kind?"

Patient: "No, I don't drink, gamble, smoke, or have any vices of any kind. I loathe smoking. In fact, I haven't any vices."

Doctor: "Well, why in the hell do you want to live another fifty years for?"

238. A preacher was preaching against the evils of alcohol. He ended his sermon by saying, "I move that every drop of wine, whiskey, beer, and alcohol of every kind and description be taken down to the river and dumped in." He stopped to catch his breath. Then he said, "And now, shall we sing that familiar old hymn, "Shall we gather at the river?"

(Bob Crocker—South Carolina)

239. Q. What do you call a dream in which dogs are biting you?

A. A bitemare.

240. Joe: "A dog bit the mailman on the leg."

Moe: "Did he put anything on it?"
Joe: "No, the dog likes it plain."

241. Q. Why do dogs like to stay at home all day?

A. Because it's a dog eat dog world out there?

242. Q. Why do some people wear their socks inside out?

A. It's because their feet get so hot that they have to turn the hose on them.
B.

243. Teacher: "Could you tell us what would have happened if Thomas Edison had not invented the electric light bulb?"

Student: "We'd be watching television by candle light."

244. Q. I have a head and a tail but no body. What am I/

A. A penny.

245. Q. What do you call a mummy that eats cookies in bed?

A. A crummy mummy.

246.   A young man took his girlfriend into a Chinese restaurant. His girlfriend was anxious to get married, but the young man was hesitant.

The waitress came to take their order. The waitress said, "How do you want your rice? Do you want it boiled or fried?"

The girlfriend replied, "Neither. I want it thrown."

247.   A preacher entered a Sunday school class while the lesson was in progress. To check on their learning, he asked the class, "Who broke down the walls of Jericho?"

A boy answered, "I didn't do it."

The preacher asked the teacher, "Is this the usual behavior in this class?"

The teacher said, "This boy is honest, and I really believe him. I really don't think he did it."

After leaving the room, the preacher sought out a deacon and explained what had happened.

The deacon said, I've known both the teacher and the pupil for years, and neither of them would do such a thing."

By this time the preacher was heartsick and reported to the Sunday school board. The chairman of the Sunday school board said, "We see no need in being disturbed. Let's pay the bill for damage to the walls and charge it to upkeep."

248.   A customer said to a druggist, "Could you give me a tablet?"

The druggist asked, "What kind?"

Customer: "A yellow one."

Druggist: "What's wrong with you?

Customer: "Nothing. I want to write a letter."

249.   Q. What is the old maid's prayer?

A. Now, I lay me down to sleep.

I wish I had a man to keep.

If there is one beneath my bed,

I hope he's heard each word I've said.

(Martha Davis—Conneaut, Ohio)

250.   Q. What is the old maid's favorite part of the Lord's Prayer?

A. The last word – AH MEN! (Amen)

251.   A motorist, following a tail light in a very dense fog, crashed into the car ahead of him when it stopped suddenly. He yelled out the window, "Why didn't you let me know when you were going to stop?"

"Why should I?" said a voice. "I'm in my own garage?"

252.   A man went into an expensive restaurant. He asked one of his friends, "Why do they call this the Rainbow Room?"

His friend replied, "When they give you the check, your face turns color."

253.   Q. "Suppose you were in my shoes. What would you do?"

A. "I'd shine them."

254.   Over-weight Biology teacher: "Sometimes a person cannot help being fat. It's in the genes."

Smart-aleck student shouts out, "In your case it's hanging over the jeans." (genes)

255.   Q. Why is a man with ten children more satisfied than a man with a million dollars?

A. Because the man with the million dollars wants more.

256.   Joe (a deckhand): "I hear that our captain has had bad luck."

Moe (a fellow deckhand): "How?"

Joe: "He married a woman, and she ran away from him. He took her for a mate, but she was a skipper."

257. Q. If you cheat on your diet, you'll gain in the end. What is the secret of dieting?

    A. Mind over platter.

258. Q. How do you know when you should go on a diet?

    A. When peeping toms ask you to go on a diet.

259. A young doctor went out West to practice his profession. An old friend met him on the street one day and asked how he was succeeding in his business.

    The doctor said, "First rate. I've had one case."

    His friend said, "Well, what was it?"

    "It was a birth," said the doctor.

    His friend asked, "How did you succeed with that?"

    The doctor spoke calmly, "Well, the woman died, and the baby died, but I think I can save the old man yet."

260. A doctor stopped at a hospital room and saw a nurse holding a man by both wrists. He said, "That's no way to check his pulse."

    The nurse replied, "I'm not checking his pulse. I'm checking his impulse."

261. A man fell out of a tall building. Through some quirk of fate, he was not killed. While he was recovering in the hospital, he was visited by a preacher. The preacher asked, "Did all the sins of your life flash through your head as you were falling?"

    "Hell no, preacher. I only fell eight stories. There wasn't enough time."

262.   Q. Why did the football player ask he coach to flood the field?"

     A. So he could go in as a sub.

263.   A man said, "My grandfather lived to be ninety five years old, and he never used glasses."

     His friend said, "He must have had good eye-sight."

     "No, he always preferred to drink from a bottle."

264.   During a college history exam before the Christmas vacation, one of the students did not know the answer to a question "What were the causes of the depression of the 1930s? (Discus each cause.)

     One of the students did not know the answer, so he wrote in his blue book, "God knows. I don't. Merry Christmas."

     In January after the Christmas vacation, the book came back with the professor's notation, "God gets 100! You get zero! Happy New Year!"

265.   Q. How do you start a flea race?

     A. One, two, flea, go.

266.   Q. What do you with a sick bird?

     A. You tweet him.

267.   Q. What do you do with a sick wasp?

     A. You take him to a wasphospital.

268.   Q. What is always coming, but never arrives.

     A. Tomorrow. When it arrives, it is today.

269.   Q. Where do owls stay while on vacation?

     A. In a hoo-tel

270.   One man said to his buddy, "Did you make up with your girlfriend?"

His buddy replied, "She said she'd meet me halfway."

The man said, "Well, that sounds pretty good."

His buddy said, "No, it's not good. She said she'd meet me halfway –She won't forgive me, but she will forget me."

271.   A woman who had eight children went to see her lawyer.

Lawyer: "What's wrong?"

Woman: "I want a divorce."

Lawyer: "Why do you want a divorce?"

Woman: "My husband does not love me."

Lawyer: "You've got eight children. Is that correct?"

Woman: "Yes."

Lawyer: "You've got <u>eight</u> children! What kind of a fix would you be in if your husband <u>did</u> love you?"

272.   Patient: "Doctor, I feel like a pack of cards."

Doctor: "Wait over there. I'll deal with you later."

273.   Two men whose boat had sunk were clinging to a raft. One of them started to pray. He said, "Oh Lord, I've broken most of the Commandments. I've been an awful sinner all my days. Lord, if you'll spare me, I'll...."

The other man shouted, "Hold on, don't commit yourself. I think I see a sail!"

274.   A man went into a restaurant. The waitress said, "What would you like to order, sir?"

The man said, "I want a bowl of chili and a few kind words."

The waitress looked about, then whispered, "Don't eat the chili."

275.   Q. Are you going to start a bakery?

A. Yes, if I can raise the dough.

276. Q. Who are the best bookkeepers?

     A. People who don't return the books they borrow.

277. Teacher: "Punctuate this sentence: Mary walked down the street."

     Boy student: "I'd make a dash after Mary."

278. Teacher: "What animal is satisfied with the least food?

     Student: "The moth. It eats nothing but holes."

279. Teacher: "There will be only a half day of school this morning."

     Students: "That's great!." They jump for joy.

     Teacher: "We'll have the other half this afternoon."

280. Student: "I wish we had lived 10,000 years ago."

     Teacher: "Why?"

     Student: "So we wouldn't have to study so much history."

281. Teacher (calls parent on the telephone): "Does your child have a behavior problem?"

     Parent: "I don't know. I've never seen him behaving."

282. Q. What is full of holes and yet holds water?

     A. A sponge.

283. Q. Why do mailmen carry letters?

     A. Letters can't walk."

284. Q. What is the difference between ants and elephants?

     A. About 2000 pounds.

285. Q. Why shouldn't you tell secrets on a farm?

     A. The corn has ears, the potatoes have eyes, and the beans talk.

286. A female oyster just returned from a date with an octopus. She was describing her date. "First he looked deep into my eyes, and then he put his arms around me, and it was just wonderful."

"What happened next?" her companion oyster asked.

A look of horror came across the oyster's face. She exclaimed, "Oh, my pearls!"

287. Miss Wilson, a young social worker, hearing that a group of refugees would be brought to a nearby church, got into car and drove to the church. Soon a truck appeared laden with people.

Clinging together at the edge of the crowd were an old man and an old woman.

"You two," Miss Wilson said. "Would you like to come home with me?'

After a quick conversation, they agreed. Miss Wilson took them to her house, gave them a good meal, and showed them to the guest room. She closed the door and went out to her living room to watch TV.

In a few moments the little old lady appeared. She said, "Thank you for your kindness. I really appreciate your being so nice, but would you be good enough to answer one question?"

"Of course," the social worker said."

"Who is this old man I'm supposed to sleep with?"

288. A patient, lying on a gurney outside the operating room, was waiting for his operation. The patient had been wondering how much the operation would cost. When his doctor showed up, he voiced his concern to the doctor.

The doctor said, "You have to be unconscious during the operation. What do you prefer -- sodium pentathol or a peak at your bill?"

289. A man said to his visitor, "These are my grandmother's ashes."

His visitor commiserated and said, "Oh, I'm sorry to hear that the poor soul has passed on."

The man said, "Passed on, hell! She's just too damn lazy to look for an ashtray."

290. A husband said to his wife, "I wish you could bake like my mother."

His wife replied, "I wish you could make dough like my father."

291. Q. What do bakers and bankers haves in common?

A. They both work with dough.

292. Q. Why couldn't the bike make it up the hill?

A. Because it's too tired. (two tired)

293. During a test, a teacher noticed that one of his students was looking at the paper of a student sitting next to him. He walked over to the student, leaned down, and whispered, "Were you copying from his paper?" The teacher pointed to the other student's paper.

The student replied, "Oh, no, sir! I was just making sure that he had mine all right."

294. Q. A Mexican fireman had two kids. He named one Jose (pronounced Hose A). What did he name the other one?

A. Hose B.

295. A young man and his girlfriend were talking together. She murmured softly, "And you say that you were in the town I was born in just last week."

"Yes," said the young man.

"And you thought of me, Bob," she cooed.

"Yes, I did," he replied calmly. "I said to myself – Isn't this where what's her name was born and raised?"

296.   On a brief holiday in town, a soldier met a young lady. One minute later he told her, "I don't know if you're going to believe this or not, but I fell in love with you at first sight."

The young lady asked, "Are you sure?"

The soldier answered, "It has to be love at first sight. I only have a four-hour pass!"

297.   An old man was walking along a country road. A young teenager in a convertible with its top down and blaring rock and roll music, stopped beside the old man. The teenager yelled, "How far is it to civilization?"

The old man replied, "Three generations."

298.   Doctor: "Mix this medicine with orange juice"

Patient: "Good idea. I hate the taste of orange juice."

299.   First man: "Did you hear Robinson snoring in church this morning?"

Second man: "Yes, I sure did. He woke me up."

300.   Q. Why does your grandmother just sit there and read the Bible all day?

A. I think she's cramming for the final.

301.   Q. What do the following have in common?

A girl who is about to be engaged.

A rabbit.

A. They both love carrots (carats)

302.   A chemistry professor was delivering a lecture. He was saying, "Oxygen is essential to all animal existence including man.

There could be no life without it. And it was discovered only two centuries ago."

Just then, one of his students raised her hand and asked, "What did they do before it was discovered?"

303.   He: (on telephone) "Say, Mabel, may I come over tonight?

She: "Sure, John, come on over."

He: "Why, this is not John."

She: "This is not Mabel, either."

304.   A new girl in school was telling her girlfriend about her first period class. She said, "I had to change my seat several times in that class."

Her girlfriend asked, "Did a man get fresh?"

The new girl smiled and said, "Well.....Finally!"

305.   A man described his marriage by saying, "We've been married almost forty years and we've had only one fight. It started the day we were married."

306.   A telephone repairman got lost in an apartment building. He went up to a lady and asked, "How do you get outside?"

She replied, "Dial 9."

307.   Q. When is a doctor most annoyed?

A. When he is out of patients (patience).

308.   Q. How were Adam and Eve kept from gambling?

A. Their pair of dice was taken from them. (paradise)

309.   Q. Why is life the riddle of all riddles?

A. Because we must all give it up.

310.   Q. Why is a baker like a beggar?

A. Because he kneads bread. (needs)

311.   Three truck drivers were at the pearly gates applying for admission to Heaven. St. Peter was interviewing them. He was asking each three questions. He turned to the first truck driver and asked, "Did you ever speed?"

"No, I never did."

St. Peter asked the first truck driver, "Did you have an overload?"

"No, I never did."

St. Peter asked the third question, "Did you ever cheat on your wife?"

"No, I never did."

St. Peter turned to the second truck driver and asked the same three questions. He received the same three answers. St. Peter then said to the second truck driver, "You wait over there with the first truck driver."

St. Peter then interrogated the third truck driver. He asked, "Did you ever speed?"

"Yes, many times. I had to speed. I had to make more money for my big family."

"Did you ever have an overload?"

"Yes, same answer. I had to make more money for my big family."

St. Peter then asked the third question, "Did you ever cheat on your wife?"

"Yes, I had two blondes in Texas and I drove to visit them as often as possible."

St. Peter then said to the first two truck drivers (who were waiting), "You two guys are liars. You go to HELL!" Then he said to the third truck driver, "You and I are going to TEXAS."

312. A man gave a book to his wife. She asked him, "What is this book about?"

     He said, "It's about the hereafter."

     His wife replied, "Why should I read it. I know what I'm <u>here after</u>."

313. Imagine one of the Marx brothers as your doctor, delivering a dose of today's high speed medicine:

     "Doc, you're charging me $50 and all you did was paint my throat."

     "What did you expect—wallpaper? Next."

     "Doc, how can I avoid falling hair?"

     "Step to one side. Next."

     "Doc, what would you take for this cold?"

     "Make me an offer. Next."

     "Doc, there's something wrong with my stomach."

     ""Keep your coat buttoned and nobody will notice. Next."

     "Doc, am I getting better?"

     "I don't know. Let me feel your purse. Next." (pulse)

314. Joe: "I understand your great uncle was the inventor of the electric shaver."

     Moe: "Yes, as a matter of fact, he's been working on it since he was a little shaver."

315. Did you know that my father has the first dollar that he ever made and that the police have the machine he made it with?

316. First man: "I didn't want to do it, but I finally got a dog for my wife."

     Second man (a joker): "Hey, good trade."

317. An inmate at an insane asylum was being interviewed by his psychiatrist. The psychiatrist was trying to find out whether the inmate should be released. The psychiatrist asked various questions. Finally he asked, "What are you going to do when you get out of this place?"

The inmate said, "I'm going to get a sling shot and break every window in this place. "The psychiatrist decided the man was not ready to be released.

Three month s later, the psychiatrist interviewed the man again and asked he same question: "What are you going to do when you get out of this place?"

The inmate replied, "I'm going to get a sling shot and break every window in this place." Again, the psychiatrist decided the man was not ready to be released.

Six months later, the psychiatrist wondered if the man should be released. He asked the same question, "What are you going to do when you get out of this place?"

I'm going to get myself cleaned up. Have a good hot bath. I'll get a haircut. I'll buy a new suit and tie. Then I'll go out and have a good dinner at a restaurant."

The psychiatrist was favorably impressed. He said, "Sounds good."

The inmate continued, "Then afterwards, I'll go to a singles' bar and pick up a good looking woman."

The psychiatrist was thinking, "This sounds normal."

The inmate continued, "Then I'm going to take her to a motel. Then I'm going to take off her blouse and her skirt and her panties. And I'm going to take the elastic band out of her panties and make myself a slingshot and come back and break every window in this place." (In memory of Avonelle Sublett)

318. A woman went to see her doctor. The doctor asked, "What's your problem?"

    "The woman said, "Last night I dreamed I was a tepee. The night before, I dreamed I was a wigwam. What's wrong with me?"

    The doctor smiled and said, "You're two tents." (too tense)

319. Two men went to an employment agency to find jobs. The counselor looked through his file and began, "How about managing a cattle breeding farm?"

    The first man objected, "That's a job for a farmer."

    The second man laughed. He stopped and said, "No, it takes a bull."

320. A stand-up comedian was being razzed. Somebody yelled, "Gee, what a ham!"

    The comedian yelled back, "I'm not a ham. A ham can be cured."

321. My great uncle committed suicide by drinking a bottle of furniture polish. It was a bad ending but a beautiful finish.

322. Man (to friend): My wife has been seeing a psychiatrist."

    Friend: "How's her mental condition now?"

    Man: "She's fine, but the psychiatrist has gone nuts."

323. Joe: "Did you hear about the new deodorant called Ventriloquist?"

    Moe: "Hell, no! What is it?"

    Joe: "It doesn't do anything for you, but it makes everybody think that the guy standing next to you stinks. It's good for use in elevators."

324. Secretary: "I'm broke. Could I have an advance payment on my salary?"

Boss: "You know, I never make advances to my secretaries."

325.   A man was trying to sell his car. The odometer had 125,000 miles on it. The car looked good but as soon as a potential customer learned about the mileage, he changed his mind.

His neighbor said to him, "Why don't you let me turn back the odometer?"

The man agreed and the neighbor turned the odometer back to 25,000 miles.

The next day, the man took the FOR SALE sign off the car and was driving it around town.

The neighbor asked, "Why don't you try to sell your car?"

The man answered, "Why should I sell this car? It's only got 25,000 miles on it."

326.   A little old lady developed a fool proof method for getting a seat on a crowded bus. Hobbling up to the nearest able body person in a seat, she's say, "Will you hold my cane so I can hold on with both hands?"

327.   A moron was filling out a physical education questionnaire form and came to the question: "Have your eyes ever been checked?"

"No," he wrote, "They've always been brown.".

328.   Q. What is the daffynition of a hypocrite?

A. A mortician who tries to look sad a $15,000 funeral.

329.   A man told a bad joke. A cynic asked, "Where did you get that Joke?"

The man replied, "Back home."

The cynic said, "That's what is called carrying a joke too far." (Some jokes go over like a lead balloon. You can't win 'em all.)

330.   Q. There were five questions on the test. Did you miss any?

A. Only the first two and the last three.

331. Tom: I lost my dog.

Joe: Did you put an ad in the newspaper?

Tom: My dog can't read.

332. Q. What did old McDonald see when he took the eye test?

A. E I E I O

333. Q. Why are you making faces at my bulldog?

A. He started it.

334. You know you are over 50 when getting a little action means your prune juice is working.

335. When you're old enough to watch your step, you're probably too old to take it.

336. Q. How fat was he?

A. He was so fat that he was not allowed on an elevator unless it was going down.

337. Always be rue to your teeth or they will be false to you.

338. A young man wrapped his arms around a shapely blond. "My darling," he breathed, "You're all the world to me. I don't know what I'd do without you. I love….."

At that moment the doorbell rang. The blond jumped up. "It's my fiancé," she gasped. "You must leave at once. Oh hurry, please hurry!"

The young man looked around nervously. "But how am I going to leave?" he asked anxiously. "I can't go out by the door. Your fiancé would see me."

The blond thought quickly. "Jump out the window," she advised.

"But, honey," he quavered. "We're on the thirteenth floor."

"So what!" she snapped back. "This is no time to be superstitious."

339. Waitress: "Do you want a roll?"

    Man customer: "No, I'll just sit here right now. What time do you get off work?"

340. Q. Did you hear about the cornflakes and the rice Crispies that had a fight?

    A. Well, I can tell you only a little at a time. It's a serial. (cereal)

341. Teacher: Use fiddlesticks in a sentence.

    Student: If you sleep in a very short bed, your fiddlesticks out. (feet will stick out)

342. "I had a fall last night which rendered me unconscious for several hours."

    "You don't mean it! Where did you fall?"

    "I fell asleep."

343. Q. What kind of pants do ghosts wear?

    A. Boo jeans. (blue jeans)

344. Jean: "That girl looks like Helen Black, doesn't she? (hell in black)

    Jane: "Why, that dress ain't black."

345. Q. What is this kleptomania that I read so much about in the newspapers? Is it catching?

    A. No, it's taking."

346. "Dear Teacher," wrote an indignant mother. "You must not whack Tommy. He is a delicate child and isn't used to it. We never hit him at home except in self-defense."

347. Teacher: What do you call the last teeth we get?

    Student: False teeth.

348. Teacher: Captain Cook made three voyages around the world. Which one did he die on?

   Student: I don't know. I've never been any good in history.

349. Father: Why does Junior have so many holes in his head? Mother: He's learning to eat with a fork.

350. In their motel room, a girl said to her boyfriend, "What's the matter? Don't you love me anymore?"

   The boyfriend replied, "You jolly well know I do. I'm just resting."

351. In the city of Berlin during World War II, a lady was running a restaurant. Because of food shortages, she was having difficulties. One day she put up a sign in her window:

   BECAUSE OF HITLER, I AM SERVING LITTLER.

   One of the Nazi officials came to visit and informed her that her servings were still too large. She put up another sign in her window:

   BECAUSE OF HESS, I AM SERVING LESS.

   Another official came to visit and said that her servings were still too large. She would have to cut down. So she decided to put up the last sign in her window:

   CLOSED. BECAUSE OF GOERING, I HAVE RETURNED TO MY FORMER PROFESSION.

   (Mrs. Martha Davis, Conneaut, Ohio)

352. A pedestrian, standing in the middle of a busy intersection, said to a policeman, "Can you tell me how to get to the hospital emergency room."

   The policeman said, "It will be soon if you stay where you are."

353. One's character is made up of what he or she does when no one is looking.

354. Q. What happens if a glass blower breathes in?

    A. He'll end up with a pain in his stomach.

355. A man jumped out of an airplane. His parachute failed to open. At 2000 feet he passed a woman coming up. He yelled to her frantically, "Do you know anything about parachutes?"

    "No," he yelled back. "Do you know anything about gas ovens?"

356. A man in a hospital was being treated for a broken leg. After putting his leg in a cast, the doctor asked him, "How do you feel?"

    The man replied, "Well, I can't kick."

357. People will doubt what you say, but they will believe what you do.

358. Q. Why did Junior rock run away from the quarry?"

    A. He was tired of being taken for granite. (granted)

359. Q. Why did two old coin collectors get together for dinner?

    A. For old dimes sake. (times)

360. Q. Why did he kangaroo see the family psychiatrist?

    A. He was feeling a little jumpy.

361. Q. When Mr. Smith died, did he leave his wife anything?

    A. No, but he left her often enough before he died.

362. Joe: "I've eaten a lot of beef and now I am as strong as an ox."

    Moe: "That's strange. I've eaten fish all my life, but I can't swim a stroke."

363. Judge (to prisoner): "I thought I told you last time I did not want to see you here again."

    Prisoner: "That's what I told the policeman, but he did not believe me."

364. Morgan went to see a psychiatrist. "Doc," he said, "I've got trouble. Every time I get into bed, I think there is somebody under it. I get under the bed, and I think there is somebody on top of it. top, under – under, top. I'm going crazy."

     "Just put yourself in my hands for two years," said the psychiatrist. "Come to me three times a week, and I'll cure you."

     "How much do you charge?"

     "A hundred dollars per visit."

     "I'll think about it."

     Morgan never went back. Six months later he met the doctor on the street. The doctor asked, "Why didn't you ever comeback to see me again?"

     Morgan snapped back "For one hundred dollars a visit! A bartender cured me for ten dollars."

     "Is that so? How?"

     "He told me to cut the legs off the bed."

365. "Doctor," she asked anxiously, "Am I finally cured?"

     "Yes, Miss Smith," replied he analyst. "I feel we have your kleptomania under control and you can go out into the world like anyone else."

     "Oh, doctor, I'm so grateful. I don't know how I can ever repay you for all you've done for me."

     "My fee is ample payment," said he analyst. "However, if you should happen to have a relapse, you might pick up one of those small cassette-type tape recorders for my son!"

366. Long before the self-sticking stamps were available, a woman went to the post office and bought a sheet of stamps. She began licking the stamps. She said to the mail clerk, "Will you help me lick these stamps?"

The mail clerk said, "No. I don't have a liquor license." (licker)

367. Epitaph: Here lies the body of Jim Lake'

    (on a tombstone) Tread softly, all who pass.

    He thought his foot was on the brake,

    But, gosh, it was on the gas.

368. He gave a very moving performance. \

    How so?

    Everyone moved to the nearest exit.

369. Did you hear about the slowest man in the world?

    How slow is he?

    He's so slow it took him an hour and a half to watch 60 minutes.

370. Q. What is a raving beauty?

    A. That's the daffynition of a girl who comes in second place in a beauty contest.

371. Q. What did the frog say after finishing his meal?

    A. Time sure is fun when you're having flies.

    (Time flies when you are having fun.)

372. Joe: Do you have any money in the bank?

    Moe: I don't know. I haven't shaken it lately.

373. Joe: Say, I've got an idea how to make the pants last.

    Moe: How?

    Joe: Make the shirt first and the pants last.

374. Tarzan came swinging into his tree house late one afternoon. "Jane," he said, "Give me a gin and tonic."

She did and he drank it down quickly. Then he said, "Give me another gin and tonic." She did and he drank it quickly again. Next, he asked for a third gin and tonic.

"Wait a minute, Tarz, "Aren't three gin and tonics too many?"

"You don't understand, Jane," said Tarzan. It's a real jungle out there.

375. The English teacher wrote on the blackboard: Let the cow be taken out of the pasture. Then she asked the class, "What mooed – active or passive—is shown here?"

The class joker raised his hand, and the teacher made the mistake of calling on him. He replied, "The cow." (mooed)

376. An employer was interviewing a man applying for a job. The employer said, "You will have to highlight your good points."

"I was fired fifteen times," said the man."

"What's good about that?" asked the employer.

"I'm no quitter."

377. Everybody says, "Pay your taxes with a smile." I tried that, but they wanted cash.

378. A college graduate got a job in a grocery store. The manager said, "Sweep the floor."

The young man said, "But I'm a college graduate."

The manager, grabbing a broom, said, "Don't let that bother you. I'll show you how."

379. 1st mother: "How are your children doing in school?"

2nd mother: "Well, I still go to PTA meetings under an assumed name."

380. Joe: "How do you expect to sell hair tonic? You don't have any hair."

Moe: "That's all right. I know a man who sells brassieres."

381. Q. What is a pop quiz in chemistry?

   A. Analyzing soda water.

382. Q. What happens when a duck flies upside down?

   A. He has a quack up. (crack up)

383. JOB WANTED: "Man, desperate and honest, will take anything."

384. FOR RENT: "Front room, suitable for two ladies, use of kitchen, or two gentlemen."

   FOR SALE: "What am I offered for a one-year-old beautiful animal, gentle, good watch dog, will eat anything and especially fond of children."

385. Q. What happened to the electrician after he jumped off the tall building?

   A. He was grounded.

386. Q. What do you call a physicist who chops a live wire with an ax?

   A. A circuit breaker.

387. Hostess: "I won't offer you a drink, Mrs. Smith, because I know you're the head of the Temperance League."

   Mrs. Smith: "Oh, no, I'm president of the Anti-Vice League."

   Hostess: "I knew there was something I shouldn't offer you."

388. A man who had once won a prize as a swimmer in the Olympics went to his local pool for a swim. He began swimming rapidly back and forth across the pool. He attracted the attention of a beautiful young lady, wearing a skimpy two-piece bikini. . When he stopped to rest and climbed out of the pool, the lady said to him, "You're really fast. Just like an Olympic swimmer."

The man said, "As a matter of fact, I was an Olympic swimmer."

At that moment, the lady dived into the pool and swam rapidly back and forth several times. The man was amazed.

When the lady climbed out of the pool, the man said to her, "Were you an Olympic swimmer, too?"

"No," the lady replied, "I was a prostitute in Venice and I worked both sides of the canal." (Dick Davis, Chicago)

389.   Prospective tenant to landlord: "Is your house a warm one?"

Landlord: "It ought to be. The painters gave it two coats recently."

390.   Q. Why is it easy to have breakfast in bed?

A. Because you can be satisfied with a few rolls and a turnover.

391.   Teacher: Us the word avenue in a sentence.

Student: I avenue baby sister. (have a new)

392.   Joe: "Did you meet your uncle at the station?"

Moe: "No, I've known him all my life."

393.   Q. When is it O.K. to drink like a fish?

A. When you drink what the fish drinks.

394.   Q. Where does a worm go in a corn field?

A. In one ear and out the other.

395.   My new girlfriend does not have much of a face, but you ought to see her neck.

396.   He: "Baby, I can read you like a book."

She: "O.K. but lay off the Braille method."

397.   Man: "I'd like to buy a flower."

Florist: "Just one?"

Man: "Yes. Just one. I am a man of few words. I like to SAY IT WITH FLOWERS."

398. 1st man: "Did you know that my brother is working with 5000 men under him?"

2nd man: "Where does he work?"

3rd man: "In a military cemetery. He mows the lawn."

399. Q. "What do you do after you finish playing post office?"

A. "Play pony express. There's more horsing around."

400. Women's faults are many. Men have only two – everything they say and everything they do.

401. Q. What roof covers the most noisy tenant?

A. The roof of the mouth.

402. Q. What is full of holes and can still hold water?

A. A sponge.

403. He: "I see in the papers that a guy ate six dozen pancakes."

She: "Oh, how waffle!" (awful)

404. Four high school boys, afflicted with spring fever, skipped morning classes. After lunch, they reported to their teacher that their car had a flat tire.

The teacher smiled, and the boys thought she was buying their story. Then suddenly she said, "Well, you missed a test this morning, so take seats apart from one another and get out your notebooks."

Still smiling, she waited for them to settle down. Then she said, "First question. "Which tire was flat—left front, right front, left rear, right rear?"

405.   A doctor was talking to a very obese patient. He said, "You are going to have to give up these intimate little dinners for two until you have another person with you."

406.   Old comedians never die. They just go to the Old Jokes Home.

407.   Question on test: Who was Cyrus McCormick?

Student's answer: Cyrus McCormick was the inventor of the McCormick reaper which did he work of one hundred men.

408.   Dad: "It's about time we had a man to man talk about the birds and the bees."

Son: "If it's all the same to you, Dad, I'd rather hear about the car and the keys."

409.   Mary took her little brother to church. He began to talk out loud during the sermon. Mary whispered to him, "Please be quiet."

"Who's going to stop me?" John asked.

Mary told him, pointing to the rear of the room, "See those men back there. They're hushers."

410.   POEM: Mary had a little lamb.

She also had a bear.

I saw Mary's little lamb,

But I never saw her bear. (bare)

411.   A guard was patrolling at a lonely outpost. He heard a sound in the bushes. He yelled, "Halt, who goes there?"

A voice yelled back, "Lady Godiva."

The guard said, "Advance and be recognized."

412.   Son: "Daddy, Mommy just ran over my tricycle."

Dad: "How many times have I told you not to leave your tricycle on the porch?"

413. Q. What do you call a person who puts you in contact with the spirit world?

    A. A bartender

414. Character is what you really are. Reputation is only what other people believe you to be.

415. Q. What are the strongest days of the week?

    A. Saturday and Sunday. Why? Because all the rest are weak days. (week)

416. Q. What did the ocean say to the shore?

    A. Nothing. It just waved.

417. Q. What kind of ghost haunts a school?

    A. The school spirit.

418. Q. Do you know why he skeleton did not go to the party?

    A. Because he had no body to go with. (nobody)

419. A man was bragging about his date of the preceding evening. She's a blonde, really great."

    He continued, "After the dance we went out and parked by the lake. I asked her for a kiss. She said she would give it to me if I put the top down, so we could enjoy the moonlight. So, I went to work and got the top down in about one hour."

    "An hour," one of his visitors exclaimed. "I got mine down in two minutes."

    "I know, but you have a convertible."

420. Joe: "Did you mark the place where the fishing was good?"

    Moe: "Yes, I put an X on the side of the boat."

    Joe: "That was stupid."

    Moe: "Why is it stupid?"

Joe: "What if next time we get a different boat?"

421.   Ted: "Tom, you are the laziest man I know. Don't you do anything quickly?"

Tom: "Yeah, I get tired fast."

422.   A young fellow at a ball game needed to go to the restroom. He left his seat and came back ten minutes later. He saw that a tall obese man was sitting in his seat. He said, "Pardon me, sir, but I think you're sitting in my seat."

The big bully sitting in the young fellow's seat said, "Prove it."

The young fellow said, "I left my pie and ice cream on the seat."

The big bully quickly stood up. The seat of his pants revealed the crushed pie and ice cream.

"Didn't you feel it when you sat down?" the young fellow asked.

"I thought it was rainwater that hadn't dried out."

The young fellow thought, *How stupid can you get? But it*

serves you right for being a big bad bully.

423.   A real estate man was quoting prices to a potential buyer--$150,000, $100,000, $80,000? The customer said, "don't you have anything for about $50,000 or less?"

"Yes, I do, the real estate man said. "Do you want to drive out and see if it is still standing?"

424.   "Old Mr. Jones won't live long. He has one leg in the GRATE," one man sitting on a bar stool said.

His listener, sitting on an adjacent bar stool, corrected him. "You mean, he has one leg in the grave."

The first man said, "No, I mean GRATE. Old Mr. Jones is going to be cremated."

425. Joe: "Who was Snow White's brother?"

     Moe: "I don't know."

     Joe: "Egg White. Get the yolk?"

426. Q. What three keys won't open doors?

     A. mon<u>keys</u>, don<u>keys</u>, and tur<u>keys</u>.

427. Q. How do you keep a camel from going through the eye of a needle?

     A. Tie a knot in its tail.

428. Q. Which elephants don't get toothaches?

     A. Those in the half of the herd that use Crest.\\

429. Teacher: "Are you animal, vegetable, or mineral?"

     Little boy: "I'm vegetable."

     Teacher: "How can that be?"

     Little boy: "I'm a human bean." (being)

430. 1st student: You flunked your test. How far were you from the correct answers?"

     2nd student: "Two seats."

431. A man was driving his car past the grounds of an insane asylum. He suddenly had a flat tire and stopped. One of the inmates behind the bars was watching him as he worked. First, he took off the wheel cover. Then he removed the six lugs and put them inside the wheel cover. Next, he removed the spare tire from his trunk. As he was rolling the tire, he accidentally bumped the wheel cover and all of the lugs went down into a drain. He didn't have any to use. He swore and said, "Dammit, what am I going to do now?"

     The inmate who had been watching him all this time from behind the bars, said "Why don't you take one lug off each of the other three tires. Use those lugs to hold your spare tire on. Then, drive to a service station or garage where you can get more lugs."

So the man followed the inmate's advice and got the spare tire fastened. Afterwards he said to the inmate, "I want to thank you for your suggestion. And, by the way, what are you doing in that insane asylum if you can figure out how to help me solve my problems?"

The inmate replied, "I'm insane and that is why I'm in here. But that does not mean I am stupid."

(David Lloyd, Cleveland, Ohio)

432.   SIGN: WATCH OUT FOR THE SCHOOL CHILDREN, ESPECIALLY IF THEY ARE DRIVING CARS.

433.   A fool and his money are welcome everywhere.

434.   If a fool and his money are soon parted, how did they get together in the first place?

435.   "I try to make my life exciting, but my wife always finds out about it."

436.   A man handed his bankbook to the teller. He said, "I want to draw out all my money."

The teller said, "Sorry, but your wife beat you to a draw."

437.   Chinese Proverb: Fool me once. Shame on you.

Fool me twice. Shame on me.

438.   She: "Lips that touch liquor shall never touch mine."

He: "Your lips?"

She: "No, my liquor."

439.   Q. What day of the year is a command?

A. March 4th. (March forth)

440.   Q. How are false teeth like stars?

        A. They only come out at night.

441.   To get maximum attention, it's hard to beat a good big mistake.

442.   Q. What happened to the kitten that ate the lemon drop? A He became a sour puss.

443.   A young man was in an automobile accident and his doctor treated him in the hospital. Afterwards the doctor made several house calls while the young man was recovering at home. During the doctor's final visit, the young man asked, "Doc, how much do I owe you?"

        The doctor named a figure.

        The young man said, "I can't thank you enough for the help you've given me."

        The doctor, seeing the man's wife enter the room, said, "Young man, you owe your fine recovery to your wife's tender care."

        The young man smiled and said, "All right, I'll make out the check to her."

444.   A lady tourist met a cowboy for the first time, and she was very curious about his costume.

        So the cowboy began explaining: "Here's my hat. It protects me from the sun. Here's my neck scarf. If a sandstorm comes up, I can put it over my mouth and nose and it protects me." Pointing to his legs, he said, "Here's my chaps. They protect my legs from friction with the horse."

        Then the lady tourist looked down at the cowboy's feet and saw that he was wearing white tennis shoes. She asked, "How come you're not wearing cowboy boots?"

        The cowboy smiled and replied, "Oh, I don't want people to think I'm a truck driver."

445.   Q. Why is it a bad thing for a husband to burn a candle at both ends?

A. It makes it twice as hard to keep his wife in the dark.

446.   Director: "Have you ever had any stage experience?

Applicant: "Well, I had my leg in a cast once."

447.   Teacher: "What was George Washington noted for?"

Student: "His memory."

Teacher: "What makes you think his memory was so great? Student: "They erected a monument to it."

448.   Q. What is the daffynition of a genilus?

A. A man who can do almost anything except make a

Living.

449.   A customer had ordered a pizza and was waiting while it was being made and baked.

After the pizza maker took it out of the oven and placed it in a box, he asked the customer, "Do you want your pizza cut into six pieces or eight pieces?"

"Six," replied the customer. "I don't believe I can eat eight."

450.   A sense of humor is the pole that adds balance as we walk the tight rope of life.

451.   Q. Why doesn't the steam locomotive sit down?

A. Because he has a tender behind.

452.   Q. Why is a haberdasher like a railroad section gang?

A. Because they both work with ties.

453.   Q. What do you call a dog with no legs?

A. A hot dog.

454.   Two detectives were investigating a murder.

1st detective: "He was shot at close range."

2nd detective: "There must have been powder marks on his body."

1st detective: "Yes, they say that is why she shot him."

455.   Q. Why don't the boy scouts make and sell cookies?

        A. Would you want to have B.S. on your cookies?

456.   Q. What is the difference between teachers and bus drivers?

        A. Teachers face their problems each day.

Bus drivers have their problems behind them.

457.   An old man was watching television. He said to his old wife, "Why don't you go out in the kitchen and get me a dish of ice cream?"

So his wife went to the kitchen. She yelled back, "Do you want a banana on it?"

"Yes," he yelled back.

"How about nuts?" his wife yelled.

"O.K., don't forget the nuts."

"How about whipped cream?" his wife yelled.

"O.K., don't forget the whipped cream?"

"How about a cherry on top?"

"O.K., don't forget the cherry on top," he yelled back.

Then, about ten minutes later, his wife came into the living room with a plate filled with a slice of ham and scrambled eggs. She handed it to him.

"Hey," the man said to his wife, "Hey, you forgot the toast."

458.   Doctor: "Your pulse is as steady as a clock."

Patient: "You've got stethoscope on my wrist watch."

459.   Q. What happened to the cat that ate a ball of yarn?

A. It had mittens instead of kittens.

460.   1st lady: "Did you know that Mrs. Smith is a very good housekeeper?"

2nd lady: "How so? I've never seen a dirtier house in all my life."

1st lady: "She's been divorced three times, and she's kept the house every time."

461.   Q. Name a great time saver.

A. Love at first sight.

462.   History teacher: "What makes the Tower of Pisa lean?"

Fat student: "I don't know, or I'd take some myself.

463.   Q. What happened when Casanova spent two days in the hospital?

A. He took a turn for the nurse. (worse)

464.   If you realize that you are not as smart today as you thought you were yesterday, you are wiser today than you were yesterday.

465.   Sign on the house of a Justice of the Peace:

ARE YOU FIT TO BE TIED?

466.   Waiter: "Do you prefer white wine or red wine?"

Diner: "It doesn't make any difference. You see, I am colorblind."

467.   The room clerk at an expensive fashionable hotel said, "I see, Mr. Jones, that you do not have a reservation. But if you are rich, you can get a room."

The indignant Mr. Jones said, "Why, I'm filthy rich!"

"If you are filthy rich, you can get a room and a bath," the clerk replied acidly.

468.   Diner (to waiter): "Yes, I know fish is brain food, but I don't care much for fish. Don't you have some other kind of brain food?"

Waiter: "Well, we do have <u>noodle</u> soup." (Use your noodle.)

469.   He: "Hey, what's that thing over the bed?"

She: "That's a canopy. You know what a canopy is?"

He: "Yes, what's the matter? Does the roof leak?"

Q. What is the difference between the canopy over the bed and the one under the bed?

A. The one under the bed is full of urine. (can of pee)

470.   A farmer was taking six ducks for a walk in the city. A policeman saw him and told him to take his ducks to the zoo.

The next day the farmer was walking down the street and the six ducks were following him again.

The policeman was angry and said, "Didn't I tell you to take those ducks to the zoo?"

The man replied, "I did and they had a great time. Now I/m taking them to the movies."

471.   A tired doctor got his wife to answer the telephone by the bed, say that he was out, and give advice which he whispered to her.

"Thank you very much, Mrs. Miller," said the voice. "But I should like to ask you one thing."

"Yes," said Mrs. Miller.

"Is that gentleman who seems to be in bed with you fully qualified?"

472.   Teacher: "Seven cows are walking along a path in a single file. Which cow can turn around and say, 'I see six pairs of horns.'?"

Student: "Why, the first cow."

Teacher: "Wrong. Cows can't talk."

473. Q. What did the Indian say when his dog fell over the cliff?
A. Dog gone.

474. Q. Why are the medieval centuries called the Dark Ages?

A. Because it was always Knight time. (night)

475. Q. What did Batman wear when he went swimming?

A. A batting suit. (bathing)

476. Q. Where did Batman plant his flowers?

A. In a batanical garden. (botanical)

477. Q. Why does Batman gargle with Listerine?

A. Because he has bat breath.

478. Q. Why does Batman walk around his house in his underwear?

A. Because he does not have a batrobe. (bathrobe)

479. Q. What did they say about Batman when he went crazy?

A. He's got bells in his batfry. (bats in his belfry)

480. Q. What did they call Batman when he worked in the state department?

A. A diplobat. (diplomat)

481. Q. Why is it a bad thing to pull the wool over someone's eyes?

A. He might see through the yarn.

482. Q. Why were 1, 2, 3, 4, 5, and 6 scared?

A. Because 7 <u>ate</u> 9. (eight)

483. Teacher: "This essay entitled <u>Our Dog</u> is, word for word, the same as your brother's. It's the same one he wrote last year."

Student: "You see, Teacher, it's the same dog."

484. A salesman dropped in to see a customer. No one was in the office except a big dog emptying waste baskets. The salesman stared at the animal, wondering if his imagination could be playing tricks.

   The dog looked up and said, "Don't be surprised, Buddy. This is part of my job."

   "Incredible!" muttered the man. "I can't believe it. I'm going to tell your boss what a prize he has in you—an animal that can talk!"

   "No, no," pleaded the dog. "Please don't! If that bum finds out I can talk, he'll make me answer the phones!"

485. A famous writer said to his doctor, "Doc, I'm having trouble with my appendix."

   The doctor replied, ""Well, use footnotes instead."

486. A football player's wife said to her two lady friends, "I hate it when my husband calls leftovers 'replays.'"

   The first lady's friend, the TV executive's wife, said, "I hate it when my husband calls them 'reruns.'" The second lady friend, the mortician's wife, said, "Be grateful. My husband refers to them as 'remains' or 'cremains.'"

487. Chemistry teacher: "What can you tell me about nitrates?" (sounds like night rates)

   Student: "They're a lot cheaper than day rates."

488. Professor: "Can you tell me anything about the great chemists of the 17th century?"

   Student: "They're all dead, sir."

489. A teacher telephoned the father of one of his failing students. The teacher asked, informally to break the ice, "Does your son burn the midnight oil?"

   The father replied, "Yes, and a lot of gasoline along with it."

490.   He: "That's a flimsy dress you're wearing."

   She: "And that's a flimsy excuse for staring."

491.   Q. What am I describing? Brick upon brick and a hole in the middle of it.

   A. A chimney

492.   Q. What is lengthened by being cut at both ends?

   A. A ditch

493.   Father: "Son, why is there a big O on your test paper?"

   Son: "The teacher ran out of stars, so she gave me a moon."

494.   Q. Why do they call it take home pay?

   A. Because there is no other place you can go with it.

495.   A high school girl was going steady with her boyfriend. Saturday night dates usually ended up in the small formal parlor of her parents' house. The young man would turn out the lights and they would talk and kiss.

   One Sunday morning the father asked his daughter, "What are the young man's intentions?"

   His daughter replied, "I don't know. He's been keeping me pretty much in the dark."

496.   A man went to his mailbox and took out the letter the mailman had just put in. He said to the mailman, "Why is this letter wet?"

   The mailman replied, "Must be postage dew!" (due)

497.   Q. Why does a baldheaded man have no use for keys?" A. Because he doesn't have any locks.

498.   She: "Are you going to the party?"

   He: "Is it formal or do we wear our own clothes?"

499. Two high school girls, between classes, were leaning against their lockers and watching the boys walking by. One girl said to the other, "Does that boy have a hole in his pants or am I seeing things?"

    The other girl answered, "Both!"

500. Q. What is a beef stew marriage?

    A. The wife is always beefing and the husband is always stewed.

501. A visitor in a hospital inquired about a patient. She asked his nurse, "Is he making any progress?"

    The nurse replied, "No. Not at all. He's not my type."

502. Q. Did you really quit smoking – cold turkey?

    A. Yes, I quit smoking cold turkey because the stuffing wouldn't stay lit.

503. Two goats were looking for something to eat. They went behind a movie theatre and found a trash can. One goat found a discarded movie film in the trash can and began eating it.

    After he finished eating it, the other goat said to him, "How was it?"

    The goat licked his chops and said, "Not bad, but the book was better."

504. A father and son were both lion trainers. One day the father disappeared completely, but the son kept his job as a lion trainer.

    One day a visitor asked the son, "Did you ever put your head inside a lion's mouth?"

    The son replied, "Only once – to look for Dad."

505. A man found that his house was infested with termites. So he hired a professional termite exterminator. After the

exterminator finished his work, he said to the home owner, "I have both good news and bad news for you."

The home owner asked, "What's the good news?"

"All of your termites are dead."

"Well, then, what can be the bad news?" asked the man.

"The bad news is –all of their relatives are coming in for the funeral."

506. You know your children are grown up when your daughter starts putting on lipstick and your son starts wiping it off.

507. A bather whose clothing was strewed

By winds that kept her quite nude

Saw a man coming along –

And unless I am wrong,

You expected this line to be lewd.

508. A tourist had visited a city in California. A native Californian asked her, "What city are you visiting?"

"San Jose," she said. She pronounced the J like a J.

The native Californian corrected her, "Oh, no," he said, "It's San Hose. In California all Js are pronounced with an H."

"Oh, I see," she said.

"By the way," the native Californian added, "When were you in San Hose?"

The lady smiled and said, "In Hune and Huly."

509. Teacher: "Did you study your history?"

Student: "No, I ain't had no time for nothin' but my English."

510. Q. What do you call a cow that has just had a calf?

A. Decaffeinated. (Bob Jack, Medina,OH)

Q. Why did the mother hen kick all the baby chickens out of the henhouse?

A. She did not want them to hear the fowl language.

(Bob Jack, Medina, OH)

511. Friend: "Did you marry her for her money?"

New Bridegroom: "They say I married her because her uncle left her a million dollars. That's not true! I would have married her regardless of <u>who</u> left her a million dollars."

512. A woman had been a prostitute all her life. She finally got married, but her husband did not know about her past history. All he knew was that she was a Protestant. He was a devout Catholic.

On their wedding night she decided to make a confession. She said, "You know, darling, I was a pro - - - - - - -." She never finished.

Her husband interrupted her by saying, "That's alright, dear. You go to your church and I'll go to mine."

513. John: "Where are you going on your vacation?"

Henry: "Yellowstone."

John: "Don't forget Old Faithful."

Henry: "Don't worry. I'm taking her with me."

514. Mother: "Were you good at church today, Dennis?"

Dennis: "Yes, a nice man offered me a big plateful of money, but I said 'No thanks.'"

515. He: "How come you aren't married?"

She: "I'm looking for the perfect man."

He: "Haven't you found him?"

She: "Yes, but he was looking for the perfect woman."

516.   As a worried son handed his bad report card to his father, he said, "Maybe I should try some other line of work."

517.   On their tenth wedding anniversary, a man said to his wife, "I'll give you your choice of gifts. You can have either a mink coat or a trip to Paris."

His wife replied, "Oh, let's take a trip to Paris. I've heard you can get real bargains on mink coats there."

518.   Q. What is the daffynition of a playboy?

A. A man who winters in Florida, summers in the Alps, and springs at blondes.

519.   "I'm a great believer in luck. I find that the harder I work, the more luck I have." (Thomas Jefferson)

520.   Jim: "How fast does your dad's car go?"

Bill: "125 miles per hour"

Jim: "I don't believe it."

Bill: "My dad's got a statement from the police that says he was going that fast."

521.   Teacher: "Give me a sentence with the word fiddlesticks in it."

Johnny: "If the bed is too short, my <u>fiddlesticks </u>out." (feet will stick out)

522.   He who hesitates is lost – as well as his parking place.

523.   Joe: "Did you hear about the clockmaker who died and left 500 clocks?"

Moe: "No."

Joe: "Now his attorneys are busy winding up the estate."

524.   A lady driving at a high speed on I-71 was pulled over by a highway patrolman. He said, "You were driving more than 90

miles per hour. Didn't you see that speed limit sign back there? It said 65 miles per hour is the speed limit."

"Yes," the lady calmly replied, "I saw that sign but I did not see you." She said to herself, "Busted1"

(Richard Murvine, Akron)

525. Q. What did the moron do after the doctor told him he had a floating kidney?"

A. He went out and had an anchor tattooed on his back.

526. A tour guide was leading group of people through a museum. "This fossil," he pointed out, "is 2 million and 9 years old."

A visitor asked, "How can you date that fossil so precisely?"

The tour guide said, "That's easy. It was 2 million years old when I came here, and I've been here 9 years."

527. GREAT AMERILCAN LIES

The check's in the mail.

I'll start my diet tomorrow.

Your money will be cheerfully refunded if you are not satisfied.

One size fits all.

I just need five minutes of your time.

It's not the money. It's the principle.

Open your mouth wide. This won't hurt a bit.

528. Alimony is like making monthly payments for a car after it has been in a wreck.

529. Daughter: "What is a second story man?"

Mother: "Your father is an example. If you don't believe his first story, he'll tell you a second story.

530.   A lady was entertaining her bridge club. Her daughter came into the room and said, "Mommy, there's a stranger in the kitchen hugging the maid."

The lady said, "Excuse me, I'll have to check."

The daughter then said, "April fool, Mommy. It's not a stranger. It's only Daddy."

531.   Q. What is the best thing to do with good advice?

A. Just pass it on to someone else. It's never of any use to you, anyhow.

532.   Q. What is he daffynition of a miracle?

A. An event described by those to whom it was told by men who did not see it.

533.   Q. What is the daffynition of illegibility?

A. A doctor's prescription written with a post office pen in the rumble seat of a secondhand car. (1920s and 1930s)

534.   Junkman: "Lady, do you have any beer bottles?"

Lady (very indignant): "Do I look like the type who drinks beer?"

Junkman: "Do you have any vinegar bottles, lady?"

535.   A job seeker woke up President Abraham Lincoln in the middle of the night. He said, "The Chief of Customs has just died. Can I have his job?"

President Lincoln groggily replied, "If it's all right with the undertaker, it's all right with me."

536.   Q. Why is prejudice a great time saver?

A. Because it enables people to form opinions without bothering with facts.

537. A family had just moved into town. The mother went to the high school to see the principal. She said to the principal, "Now, I want my son to have a thoroughly modern and up-to-date education – including Latin."

The principal said, "Yes, of course, though Latin is, as you know, a dead language."

"That's all the better," the mother said, "my son is going to be an undertaker."

538. An intoxicated husband came home very late one night. He and his cronies had visited several night clubs.

His wife said, "Why are you so late?"

"I was playing...golf," he uttered.

His wife exclaimed, "At two o'clock in the morning?"

"I was...using...night...clubs," he managed to verbalize and laughed hilariously.

539. Tom: "My brother fell off a ten story building."

Jim: "Was he injured?"

Tom: "No. He fell through a manhole into the subway and was killed by an underground train." (Tain't funny, Magee.)

540. Q. Did you hear about the lady that got married four times?

A. First she married a banker, Second, she married an actor, Third, she married an embalmer, and Fourth, she married an undertaker.

Q. What's an easy way to remember this joke?

A. One for the money, two for the show, three to get ready and four to go.

541. Teacher: "Name two pronouns, Tommy."

Tommy: (caught unprepared). "Who? Me?"

542. Q. What is the only thing lost by politeness?

A. A seat on a crowded bus.

543. Q. Why is a bad pencil like a bad joke?

A. Because it has no point.

544. Mother: "Straighten out your room."

Billy: "It isn't crooked."

545. Q. What does a farmer grow if he works hard?

A. Tired.

546. Tommy: "Can you fool your mother?"

Johnny: "No. Fooling my mom is like trying to sneak a sunrise past a rooster."

547. Q. What is the biggest diamond in the world?

A. A baseball diamond.

548. Q. Why were the Indians the first people in North America?

A. Because they had reservations. (Tain't funny, Magee)

549. Q. What do you call a duck that gets all As?

A. A wise quacker.

550. Psychiatrist:: "What's wrong?

Patient: "I have the same disturbing dream night after night."

Psychiatrist: "Describe the dream."

Patient: "There's this big monster that is chasing me and just as he is about to catch me, my alarm clock goes off and I escape. What can I do to stop this from happening?"

Psychiatrist: "Don't forget to set your alarm clock."

551. Mother: "Did you eat all the cookies, Tom?"

Tom: "No."

Mother: "But there is only one left."

Tom: "That's the one I did not eat."

552.   Diner (in restaurant): "Do you serve crabs here?'

Waiter (smirking): "Yes, madam, we'll serve you."

553.   Customer: "I'd like to see something cheap in a straw hat."

Clerk: "Certainly, sir. Try this one on, sir. And the mirror is on your left."

554.   Did you hear about the waterbed sales where they were flooded with calls?

555.   Did you hear about the couple who got a waterbed and then drifted apart?

556.   Q. Did you get the check I sent you?

A. Yes, I got it twice. Once from you and once from the bank.

557.   Mrs. Centipede: "We're going to have to mortgage the house again, dear."

Mr. Centipede: "Why?"

Mrs. Centipede: "The children need shoes."

558.   Joe: "I've solved the mystery of what a hotel means when it advertises rooms for $5.00 and up."

Moe: "What is it?"

Joe: "I got one of the five dollar rooms and I was up all night."

559.   A truck driver was sitting at a counter in a restaurant eating his lunch. Three Hell's Angels guys wearing black leather jackets swaggered in and stood next to the truck driver. One picked up the truck driver's sandwich and took a bite out of it. Another picked up his cup of coffee and drank some of it. The third one took a bite out of his pie.

The truck driver did not say anything, and finally the three Hell's Angels went to a booth in the back of the restaurant.

The truck driver picked up his bill, paid it, and walked out the door of the restaurant.

After the truck driver left, the counterman said to the waitress, "He's not much of a man, is he?"

The waitress ran to the window and yelled back, "He's not much of a truck driver either. He just ran over three motorcycles."

560.   Joe: "Did you hear about the restaurant on the moon? It went out of business."

Moe: "Why?"

Joe: "It had great food but no atmosphere."

561.   Q. Why is the funeral business so profitable?

A. People are just dying to get in.

562.   Q. When do rabbits have sixteen legs.

A. When there are four of them.

563.   A blind man had a seeing eye dog. He suddenly picked up the dog by the tail and started swinging the dog around.

A man standing nearby said to the blind man, "Why are you swinging your dog by the tail?"

The blind man said, "That's so I can see in all directions."

564.   Q. What is an optimist?

A. An optimist is a man who thinks his wife has quit smoking cigarettes when he finds cigar butts in the house.

565.   Did you say that the man was shot in the woods, doctor?

No, I said he was shot in the lumbar region. (lumber)

566. A good looking and sexy young woman had just been hired as a secretary.

    Two of the older women employees were discussing her at lunch One said, "Why did they hire her as a secretary. She can't spell."

    The other said, "Casting a spell is her strong point."

567. Q. Why was the baby strawberry sad?

    A. Because his parents were in a jam

568. Q. Why are elephants wrinkled?

    A. Did you ever try to iron one?

569. New boss: "I hope that punctuation is your strong point."

    Secretary: "I always get to work on time."

570. CRAZY PUNS

    Where can a man buy a cap for his knee?

    Or a key to a lock of his hair?

    Can your eyes be called an academy because there are two pupils there?

    What jewels are in the crown of your head?

    Who walked the bridge of your nose? Can you do the shingling in the roof of your mouth

    With the nails on the ends of your toes?

    Can the crook of your elbow be sent to jail?

    If so, what did it do?

    Can you sit in the shade of the palm of your hand?

    Be darned if I know, do you?

    Did you ever sharpen your shoulder blades?

Can you beat the drum in your ears?

Do the calves in your legs eat the corn on your toes?

Then why not grow corn on the ears? (anonymous)

571. An employer was interviewing a job applicant. He said, "I want to hire a man who is responsible."

The job applicant replied, "I'm just the man you want. Everywhere I've worked, every time something went wrong, they said I was responsible."

572. Q. A naked lady sat down on a cane bottomed chair. After the lady got up, what did the chair say to the lady?

A. Well, I certainly made an impression on you.

573. A young man had just given a diamond engagement ring to a young lady. The young lady turned up her nose and said, "You got fooled on this so-called diamond ring."

The young man said, "I guess not. I know my onions."

"But not your carrots," she replied. (carats)

Q. What do new brides and rabbits have in common?

A. They both love carats. (carrots)

574. Q. How can you tell the sex of a chromosome?

A. You pull down its genes. (jeans)

575. Q. Why did the moron bring a ladder to a football game? A. He wanted to see the Giants play.

576. Teacher: "Johnny, did your father write this story?"

Johnny: "No, he started it, but Mom had to do it over."

577. Teacher: "Give me a sentence using the word POLITICS in it."

Student: "A parrot named Polly swallowed a watch, and now POLLY TICKS."

578. Irate father: "I'll teach you to kiss my daughter!"

    Daughter's boyfriend: "You're too late. I've already learned."

579. Sunday school teacher: "Can any of you give me a commandment with only four words in it"

    A hand was raised immediately. The teacher said, "Yes, Ben, you may answer."

    Ben laughed and said, "KEEP OFF THE GRAS.

580. Behind every great man is his mother.

    Mrs. Morse: "Sam, stop tapping your fingers on the table. It's driving me crazy."

    Mrs. Lindbergh: "Charles, can't you do anything by yourself?"

    Mrs. Washington: "George never did have a head for money."

    Mrs. Armstrong: "Neil has no more business taking flying lessons than the man on the moon."

581. Q. Why is it dangerous to work outdoors in the spring time?

    A. The grass is full of blades. The trees are shooting. Every flower has a pistil, and the bulrush is out. (bull rushes out)

582. Q. Why was Ben Franklin surprised when the lightning hit the key on his kite?

    A. He found it shocking.

583. Q. How do you make holy water?

    A. Fill a teakettle with water. Take it to the stove and boil the hell out of it.

584. Q. What length were women's skirts in colonial times? .

    A. A little above two feet.

585. Teacher: "Jimmy, why don't you wash your face? I can see what you had for breakfast this morning."

Jimmy: "What was it?"

Teacher: "Eggs."

Jimmy: "Wrong, Teacher. That was yesterday morning."

586.   Q. I have a head and a tail. Nothing else. What am I?

A. A penny or a coin.

587.   Q. I speak every language, but I never went to school. What am I?

A. An echo.

588.   Q. I have no feet, but I <u>wear</u> shoes. What am I?

A. A sidewalk

589.   Doctor: "There goes my best friend."

Neighbor: "Are you going to marry her?"

Doctor: "Can't afford to. She's my best patient."

590.   A superintendent of schools was interviewing a young lady who had applied for a teaching position. He asked her, "How long do you plan to teach school?"

She replied, "From here to maternity."

591.   In the long run the pessimists may be proved right, but the optimists have a better time on the trip.

LIFE IS A MYSTERY TO BE LIVED, NOT A PROBLEM TO BE SOLVED.

592.   Superstition is childish, immature, and irrational, but how much does it cost to knock on wood?

593.   Wife: "Could you give me ten dollars?"

Husband "Last week it was twenty dollars. The other day it was thirty dollars. What are you doing with all this money?"

Wife: "Nothing yet. You haven't given me any."

594. Once there was a church which did not have a bell ringer, so the priest asked the congregation if anyone would like to do it. A man without arms offered to do the job.

Well, every day during mass, this man would walk up to the altar and ring the bell with his face.

One day the man fell down and was knocked unconscious. The priest and many people stood around and were very concerned.

The priest, elderly and forgetful, had forgotten about this man's job. He asked the people, "Does anyone know who this man is?"

Somebody replied, "I don't know his name, but his face rings a bell."

595. Before his sermon, a preacher was giving instructions to his organist. He said, "After I say—Will all those people who will contribute $20.00 toward the mortgage <u>please stand</u>? -- play something appropriate."

The organist asked, "What is appropriate?"

The preacher said, "The National Anthem."

596. In a crowded theatre a heavy set man got up from his seat and stumbled over the fee of several people on his way to the aisle. He bought a box of popcorn and returned, but he did not remember what row he was in.

He went to the suspected seat and leaned over and asked the person in the aisle seat, "Did I step on our feet when I went out?"

The person angrily replied, "You sure did!"

The heavy set man said, "This is the right row then."

597. 1st moron: "What keeps the moon from falling to the earth?"

2nd moron: "It must be the beams."

598. Q. Why is a room full of married people empty?

   A. Because there is not a single person in it?

599. Q. What is the difference between a flea and an elephant?

   A. An elephant can have fleas, but a flea can't have elephants.

600. Here are a few famous last words:

   "Give me a match. I think my gas tank is empty."

   "Let's see if it's loaded."

   "I don't need to study anymore."

601. Q. What did the artist's model say to the artist?

   A. I don't feel in the nude for work, somehow.

602. It isn't the cough that carries you off. It's the coffin they carry you off in.

603. Q. When is dough like the sun?

   A. When it rises, it is light.

604. Q. Why do white sheep eat more than black ones?

   A. Because there are more of them.

605. Q. Where are happiness and contentment always to be found?

   A. In the dictionary.

606. A man sent away for a course in mental telepathy. He did not receive anything in the mail. So he telephoned the company. He said, "Hey, I ordered that course in mental telepathy, and I haven't gotten it yet in the mail."

   The company man said, "We don't send out that course in the mail. We send it in a different way. We send it by mental telepathy."

   The customer said, "But I didn't receive anything."

   The company man said, "I know. You are flunking the course."

607. Playgirl: What's cooking?

 Playboy: Chicken, want'a neck?

608. Q. What do you call a bull that falls asleep a lot?

 A. A bulldozer.

609. Q. What did the bubble gum say to the shoe?

 A. Boy, am I stuck on you?

610. Q. What kind of an animal belongs in a classroom?

 A. A bookworm.

611. Lulu: "I don't like this picture of myself."

 Bubu: "Why not?"

 Lulu: "It does not do me justice?"

 Bubu: "You don't want justice. You want mercy."

612. A mother and son, Johnny, were riding on a crowded bus. They had seats, but there were many people standing.

 During the ride Johnny peeled a banana and ate it.

 After mother and Johnny got off the bus, Mother said, "Johnny, that was very tidy and thoughtful of you not to throw your banana peeling on the floor of the bus. By the way, what did you do with it?"

 Johnny said calmly, "I put it in the coat pocket of the man standing next to me."

613. Q. Why did the baker stop making donuts?

 A. He was tired of the hole business. (whole)

 Q. Why did the moron plant Cheerios in his back yard. A. He wanted to grow donuts.

614. A minister was performing a marriage ceremony. He said, "If anyone can show just cause why this man and this woman

should not be joined together in holy matrimony, let him speak now or forever hold his peace."

The nervous bridegroom said, "Please, sir, if you are not careful, you'll talk her out of it."

615.   615. "Always remember to forget the things that make you sad. And always remember to remember the things that make you glad." (Elbert Hubbard)

616.   Christmas is the time of year you exchange hellos with strangers and good <u>buys</u> with friends.

617.   Mary had just one date with her new boyfriend. She was discussing him with her mother.

Mother said, "Your boyfriend seems very bashful."

"Bashful! "Bashful is no name for it."

Mother tried to be helpful. She said, "Why don't you encourage him a little more? Some men have to be taught how to do their courting. He's a good catch."

"Encourage him! He can't take the most obvious hint. Why, only last night when I sat all alone on the sofa, he perched up in a chair as far away as he could get. I asked him, 'Don't you think it's strange that a man's arm and a woman's waist seem always to be the same length? What do you think he did?"

"Why, just what any sensible man would have done—tried it. He put his arm around your waist, didn't he?"

"No," her daughter said, "He asked me if I could find a piece of string and a yardstick. He wanted to make measurements and see if it was true."

618.   I sneezed a sneeze into the air.

It fell to ground I know not where.

But hard and cold were the looks of those

In whose vicinity I snooze.

619. Q. Why is a baker like a beggar?

   A. Because he kneads bread (needs)

620. Q. When is a doctor most annoyed?

   A. When he is out of patients. (patience)

621. Q. Why is life the biggest riddle of all riddles?

   A. Because we must finally give it up.

622. Q. What is a three letter word used by more than a few

   To make people think they know more than they do? A. Etc.

623. A man from a northern state says, "In my state the winds are so powerful, they blow people right out of their houses."

   A man from Texas says, "That's nothing. In my state the winds sometimes blow two or three days out of the week."

624. Mabel: "Have you heard I'm engaged to an Irish boy?

   Violet: "Oh, really!"

   Mabel: "No, O'Riley."

625. Joe: "There's a new drink out called the David and Goliath cocktail."

   Moe: "Why is it called that?"

   Joe: "One small one and you're stoned."

626. Teacher: "What would happen if you did not have ears?

   Johnny: "I wouldn't be able to see."

   Teacher: "Why?"

   Johnny: "My glasses would fall off."

627. Q. Why do Indians call white men –pale face? (pail)

A. One of the men on the Mayflower was so homely that Pocahontas had to put a bucket over his head before she'd even get close to him. Ever since that time, Indians have been calling their white brothers <u>pail</u> face (pale)

628. There was a 95 year old man in a nursing home who did not have any teeth.

One day he had two visitors. On the table next to the old man was a bowl of peanuts.. The visitors knew that the old man did not have any teeth and figured he could not eat the peanuts. So the visitors helped themselves and ate all the peanuts.

When it was time to leave, one of the visitors said to the old man, "We're sorry we ate all your peanuts, but you couldn't eat them anyway—since you don't have any teeth."

The old man said, "That's O.K. Before you got here I sucked off all the chocolate."

629. Q. Why should soldiers be tired on the first day of April? A. They have just had a 31 day march.

630. 1st driver: "You say that you have driven a car for twenty years and never had a complaint from a back seat driver. How can that be?"

2nd diver. "Easy. I dive a hearse."

631. 1st lady: "I've been married four times Do you think I am a loose woman?"

2nd lady: No, dearie, you're just a busy body."

632. Joe: "The doctor said he'd have me on my feet in two weeks?"

Moe: "And did he?"

Joe: "He sure did. I had to sell my automobile to pay the bills."

633. Teacher: "In what part of the world are the most ignorant people found?"

Student: "In New York City."

Teacher: "Where did you get that information?"

Student: "Well, the geography book says that's where the population is the most dense."

634. Joe: "Did you hear about the moron family that froze to death at the drive-in theatre?"

Moe: "No. How did it happen?"

Joe: "They went to see CLOSED FOR THE SEASON."

635. Give two daffylnitions of a diplomat:

(1) A man who remembers his wife's birthday but not her age

(2) A man who can tell another man to go to hell and say it in such a nice way that he wants to get a head start.

636. A man was on a golf course and saw a funeral procession going by. He took off his hat and. held it over his heart. Someone asked him, "Do you know who died?"

The man said, "Yeah, my wife."

637. Doctor: "I've got both good news and bad news for you. The good news is that you've got 24 hours left to live."

Patient: "What's the bad news?"

Doctor: "The bad news is – I tried to call you yesterday."

638. "Joe: "Do you know what they call the man who doesn't believe in birth control?"

Moe: "No. What?"

Moe: "Daddy."

639. A pilot had three passengers with him in his small airplane. The passengers were a politician, a priest, and a boy- scout. Suddenly the plane had engine trouble, and the pilot said they would have to bail out. He said, "We've got only three

parachutes, and I'm taking one of them. I've got seven children and I'm the bread winner in my family." Then the pilot bailed out.

The politician said, "I'm the greatest politician in the world. I have to save humanity." The politician bailed out.

Then the priest said to the boy-scout, "There's only one parachute left. You take it. You've got your whole life before you, and mine is almost over anyway."

The boy-scout said, "No, we've each got a parachute. That greatest politician in the world bailed out with my knapsack."

640. A man said to his girlfriend, "If you don't marry me, I'll get a rope and hang myself right in front of your house."

"Oh, please don't do that," pleaded the girl. "My father doesn't want you hanging around here anymore."

641. A man said to a sales lady in a jewelry store, "I'd like an engagement ring."

Saleslady: "How mulch do you want to spend?"

Man: "About $150."

Saleslady: (brings out a tray). "These are our CAN HARDLY brand."

Man: "What does CAN HARDLY mean?"

Saleslady: "Can hardly see 'em."

642. Teacher: "What is a Laplander?"

Sudent: "That is a person who loses his balance on a bus." (lap lander)

643. Friend: "What's the matter with your wife? Is she sad?"

Husband: "Yes. She's had a great shock."

Friend: "What happened?"

Husband: "She was helping at a garage sale, and she took off her new $10 hat and laid it down. A couple of hours later she found out that somebody had sold it for 50 cents."

644. A 95 year old man with 20-20 vision applied for a job as a golf caddy. He got the job.

The first day on the job, the golfer asked him, "Where did my ball go?"

The 95 year old man with 20-20 vision replied, "I don't remember."

645. A lady named Helen Hunt found a set of keys in a hotel lobby. She immediately said to a bellhop, "I found these keys. What shall I do with them?"

The bellhop grabbed a microphone and announced loudly, "If anyone lost their keys..." And then he turned toward the lady, "What's your name?"

The lady replied, "Helen Hunt."

The bellhop returned to his microphone, "If anybody has lost their keys, go to Helen Hunt for them." (hell and hunt)

646. Q. Why wouldn't the skeleton cross the road?

A. He didn't have the guts.

647. Moe: "We were so poor we could not afford a watch dog."

Joe: "We stayed awake all night and barked ourselves."

648. Two athletic club members were in the locker room. As they started to undress, one man saw that the other man was wearing a girdle. Surprised, he asked, "How long have you been wearing a girdle?"

The other man answered, "Ever since my wife found it in the glove compartment of my car."

649. Boy: "Are you going to be busy tonight?"

Girl: "I don't know. This is our first date."

650. And this is good old Boston town,

The Home of the bean and the cod

Where the Lowells talk only with the Cabots,

And the Cabots talk only with God.

651. Mary: "Did you go to the doctor the other day?"

John: "Yes, I did."

Mary: "And did he find out what you had?"

John: "Very nearly."

Mary: "What do you mean – very nearly?"

John: "Well, I had $50 in my wallet, and he charged me $49."

652. Joe: "I saw the doctor today about my loss of memory."

Moe: "What did he do?"

Joe: "He made me pay in advance."

653. Ethan: "Did you hear about the farmer who bundled all of his hay into square bales?"

Ryan: "No. Why? Most farmers make round bundles."

Ethan: "Because he wanted all of his cows to get a square meal."

654. Tyler: "Did you hear the story about the sword swallower?"

Ethan: "No."

Tyler: "The sword swallower from the carnival went into a sewing store to buy pins and needles."

Ethan: "Why did he want pins and needles?"

Tyler: "Because he was on a diet."

655.   Teacher: "Define euthanasia."

Student: "Young people in Asia." (Youth in Asia)

656.   Q. What do you call a man who shaves 20 times a day?

A. A barber

657.   A moron applied for a job as a deputy sheriff. The examiners asked him a question, "What days of the week start with a T?"

The moron replied, "Today and Tomorrow."

"No," the examiners told him. "Go home and study."

The next day he came back and applied for the job again. The examiners asked him, "Who killed Abraham Lincoln?"

The moron replied, "I don't know."

"Go home and study."

When he got home his wife asked, "Did you get the job?"

He replied, "I guess so. They've got me working on a murder case already."

658.   Joe: "Your assets seem alright. What about your liabilities?"

Moe: "I can lie with the best of them."

659.   Q. What color is the sun and the wind?

A. The sun rose and the wind blue. (screwy!)

660.   Q. What is the healthiest animal in the world?

A. The ant eater. Because he is full of antibodies.

(ants' bodies)

661.   The behavior of some children suggests that their parents embarked on the sea of matrimony without a paddle.

662.   Wife: "Why can't we take that ocean cruise?

Husband: "With the cost of living going up, beggars can't be cruisers." (Beggars can't be choosers.)

663.   Q. What do animals do when they lose their tails?

A. Go to a retail store.

664.   Q. Why is a coward like a leaky faucet?

A. They both run.

665.   Teacher's comment about a student with problems: "Not only is he the worst behaved child in school, he also has a perfect attendance record."

666.   Two ladies were sitting on a sofa in a hotel lobby watching the passing parade of people.

One lady said, That woman who just walked by was wearing a $12,000 fur coat. I saw it in the store window just last week."

The other lady said, "Wouldn't it be foolish for someone to pay that much for a fur coat?"

"Yes, but I hope to find him someday," the first lady said.

667.   Q. "Did you hear about the guy who ate 79 pancakes?"

A. "Oh, how waffle!"

668.   Jack: "Did you hear that the astronauts found some fossil bones on the moon?"

Mike: "I guess the cow didn't make it."

669.   Now I lay me down to sleep.

The film is long and the subject is deep.

If it should end before I wake,

Someone kick me for goodness sake.

(The Sleepy Student's Prayer)

670. A man got a job at a zoo. He had the job of taking care of the bears. There were all kinds of bears—Kodiak bears, brown bears, black bears, polar bears, grizzly bears. When a bear got out of hand, he had to drop a noose over the bear's head and pull it out of the cage.

     He got tired of this job and applied for another job. At the interview he was asked, "Why did you quit your last job?"

     He replied, "I got tired of being the nooser of bad bears."

     (bearer of bad news)

671. BUMPER STICKER: If you don't like the way I drive, get off the sidewalk.

     BUMPER STICKER: If you can read this, you're too damn close.

     BUMPER STICKER: Honk if you love Jesus.

672. A man bought a large antique clock at an antique store. He left the store, carrying this large clock down the sidewalk.

     A drunk bumped into him and knocked the clock to the sidewalk.

     The man yelled, "Hey, watch where you're going!"

     The drunk yelled back, "Why don't you wear a wrist watch like everybody else?"

673. Q. A duck went into a drug store. He got the chap stick. What did he say to the clerk?

     A. Put it on my bill.

674. Caitlyn: "A snake snapped at me."

     Ethan: "Snakes don't snap. They strike."

     Caitlyn: "This one was a garter snake."

675. Q. What were Tarzan's last words?

A. Who greased the grapevine?

676. Q. What begins with an E and ends with an E and has a letter in between?

A. An envelope.

677. Q. What is the difference between a hill and a pill?

A. One's hard to get up. The other's hard to get down.

678. Tyler: "Did you hear the rope joke?"

Ethan: "No."

Tyler: "Skip it."

679. Q. What did the moron say when he poured coke into his gas tank?

A. Things go better with coke.

SIGN ABOVE A URINAL: The hell with coke! This is the

Pause that refreshes.

680. The following joke dates back to the 1930s when the WPA was in existence: A man had been working on a construction job for two weeks and had not been given a shovel yet. He went to see his foreman about this.

The foreman said, "What are you complaining about? You've gotten your paycheck, haven't you?"

The man said, "Yes, but all the other guys have something to lean against."

681. Q Why did Mickey Mouse take a trip to outer space?

A. To find Pluto.

682. Susie: "Is that a real diamond ring?"

Marge: "If it isn't, I've been cheated out of my ninety-nine cents."

683.   Mama Owl: "I've worried about Junior Owl."

Papa Owl: "What's the matter with him?"

Mama Owl: "Well, lately, he just doesn't give a hoot about anything."

684.   A pair of slick counterfeiters made perfect $18.00 bills. But they did not know what to do with them.

Finally one of the counterfeiters said, "Let's take them to a country store—way out in the boondocks—where people are dumb."

So they did.

They said to the store clerk, "Could you give us change for this bill?"

The store clerk looked at it and said, "Would you like the change in two <u>nine</u> dollar bills or three <u>six</u> dollar bills?

685.   Q. What is the slogan for pornographic movie producers?

A. This is the dawn of a nude day.

686.   Q. How does a checkered career often end?

A. In a striped suit.

687.   Q. What would happen if all the students who sleep in class were laid end to end?

A. They would be much more comfortable.

688.   Q. What's wrong with having a wonderful summer vacation?

A. The bigger the summer vacation, the harder the fall.

689.   Sunday school teacher: "Why in your prayers do you only ask for your daily bread instead of asking enough for a week?"

Little boy: "So we can get it fresh every day."

690.   Joe: "Sally must be a wild girl."

Moe: "Why is that?"

Joe: "I heard her father say he could hardly keep her in clothes."

691. Little boy: "The people next door must be poor."

Mother: "What makes you think so?

Little boy: "They made such a fuss about their baby swallowing a quarter."

692. Q. Why does Cinderella hate baseball games?

A. Because she ran away from the ball.

693. A little old lady developed a foolproof method for getting a seat on a crowded bus. Hobbling up to the nearest able-bodied person in a seat, she'd say, "Will you hold my cane so I can hold on with both hands?"

694. Q. What becomes of love triangles?

A. Most of them turn into wreck tangles? (rectangles)

695. Now I lay me down to sleep. (The Old Maid's Prayer)

I wish I had a man to keep.

If there is one beneath my bed,

I hope he's heard each word I've said.

696. He: "Baby, I can read you like a book."

She: "O.K., but lay off that Braille method."

697. Casanova: My new girlfriend does not have much of a face, but you ought to see her neck.

698. Q. What's cooking?

A. Chicken. Want a neck? (wanna neck)

699. A doctor told his wife that he would not be able to go with her on their scheduled trip to Europe. He explained, "The doctor

who was supposed to replace me can't do it. But you go ahead anyhow for the three week trip to Europe.

So his wife decided to take the trip to Europe without her husband.

Now the doctor had a very sexy and beautiful receptionist. When this receptionist reported to work the next day, she found a gift from the doctor's wife. It was a beautiful basket. It contained <u>twenty-one</u> apples.

(An apple a day keeps the doctor away.)

700.   "What should I take, Doctor," gasped the tense patient, "when I'm run down?

"Try the license plate number first," replied the tired doctor. "Then get the make the car."

701.   A moron was trying to light a match. He struck the first match. It didn't work, so he threw it away. Then he tried the second match. It didn't work either, so he threw it away.

He then struck the third one and it lit up. He then quickly blew it out and said, "That's a good one. I've got to save it."

702.   Mr. Jones: "Do you think your son will forget all he has learned in college?"

Mr. Smith: "I hope so. He can't make a living necking."

703.   The proud mother said to her child's teacher, "Tommy is a genius. He has many original ideas, doesn't he?"

"Yes," replied the teacher, "especially when it comes to spelling."

704.   The doctor prescribed exercise for the busy executive's wife. After three days, the doctor asked, "Is she exercising?"

"She's jumping and she's running," said the executive.

"Oh," said the doctor. How much of this does she do each day?"

"Lots," said the executive. "She's jumping to conclusions and running up bills."

705.   Joe: "What did your prof give you in math?"

Moe: "I flunked. He said I didn't know math from a hole in the ground."

706.   Little Johnny was in the first grade. He came home from school one day, and his father fixed him an after school snack—a bowl of Wheaties. While his son was eating, the father sat down across the table.

When his son had finished, he asked, "What did you learn in school today??"

Johnny replied, "Two plus two, the son of a bitch is four." The father was flabbergasted. "Did your teacher really say—two plus two, the son of a bitch is four?"

"Yes," and Johnny repeated it. "Two plus two, the son of a bitch is four."

The father was very disturbed. He telephoned the teacher and angrily asked her, "Why are you using these swear words in class?"

The teacher said, "I never swear."

"My son Johnny just told me that you said –two plus two, the son of a bitch is four."

"OH – that!" The teacher laughed. "I said 'two plus two, the sum of which is four.'"

707.   When Judy got to be 28 years old without any prospects of getting married, her mother nagged her into inserting an ad in a matrimonial paper. The ad read: "Beautiful, exotic young heiress seeks correspondence with devil-may-care gentleman who wants to go places fast."

After the ad appeared, the mother asked anxiously, "Well, any answers?"

"Just one." The daughter sighed.

"Who wrote it?" demanded the mother.

"I shouldn't tell you," said the daughter.

"But this was my idea," shouted Mama, and I insist upon knowing."

"All right," said the daughter. "You asked for it. It was from Papa."

708.   Doctor: "The best thing that you can do is to get back to work immediately."

Patient: "Will that help my condition."

Doctor: "Well, no. But at least you'll be able to pay me."

709.   The elderly farm couple sat in their rocking chairs in front of the fireplace one wintry night in Montana.

"The years are passing us by, Hannah," said the old man.

"Yes," she agreed.

"We're getting older," he said, "And pretty soon only one of us will be left."

"That's right," she said. "And when that happens, I'm moving to California."

710.   Q. What did the baby porcupine say when he backed into the barbed wire fence?

A. Is that you, Mama?

711.   Teacher: If I take a potato and divide it into two parts, then into four parts and each of the four parts into two parts, what would I have?

Student: Potato Salad

712.   Q. How can a man get into trouble by being frank and earnest?

A. He was Frank in New York and Ernest in Chicago.

713.   Q. What has four eyes (I's) and can't see?

A. Mississippi.

714.   On a busy New York City street a taxicab was barely crawling along. A lady passenger in the back seat said to the cab driver, "Can't you go any faster?"

The driver replied, "I can, lady, but I have to stay with the cab."

715.   Employer: "It'nine o'clock. You should have been here at eight o'clock."

Employee: "I fell out of an eight story building."

Employer: "You mean it took you an hour to fall eight stories."

716.   Joe: "This liniment makes my arm smart."

Moe: "Why don't you rub some on your head?"

717.   Small boy: "I say, Dad, my teacher said this morning that the law of gravity keeps us on the earth. Is that right?"

Dad: "Yes, my boy, that is correct."

Small boy: "Well, how did people get on the earth before that law passed?"

718.   A professor in a medical college was introducing a guest speaker to his students. He exclaimed, "Today, students, we are honored to have in our midst the oldest practicing physician in the country." He turned toward the guest speaker and said, "Now, doctor, don't you have a few wise words for these medical students?"

After being helped to his feet and pondering a few minutes, the old gentleman gave the following shaky reply: "Always scribble your prescriptions illegibly – and write your bills clearly."

719. Tom: "What church do you belong to?"

    John: "None."

    Tom: "Well, what church do you go to when you do go?"

    John: "If you must know, the church which I stay from most of the time when I don't go is the Baptist".

720. Ethan: "How many men does it take for a funeral?"

    Ryan: "I don't know."

    Ethan: "It takes seven."

    Ryan: "Why seven?"

    Ethan: "Six to carry the casket and one to carry the chair."

    Ryan: ""What's the chair for?"

    Ethan: "For Rigor Mortis to set in."

721. A man took his wife to see a doctor. After the doctor examined her, the man asked, "Does my wife have the Russian flu?

    "No," the doctor said, "She's got the Egyptian flu."

    "What's the Egyptian flue?"

    The doctor said, ""She's going to be a mummy."

722. Q. What is the daffynition of conscience?

    A. Something that feels terrible when everything else feels good.

723. Every man is a born collector. First, he collects beetles, toads, and marbles; then girls, kisses, and fancy ties; then dollars, troubles, and a family; then jokes, stories, and letters; and lastly, aches, symptoms, and memories.

724. A girl who was recently engaged to the office Romeo went to a wedding shower.

When she got home, her mother said, "I guess you got some raves about your ring!"

"Yes," her daughter said. "In fact, a few of the office girls recognized it."

725. Joe: "We're so poor I don't have any good pants to wear. Mine are all raggedy and full of holes."

Moe: "What about Jean's?"

Joe: "Hers don't fit me either." (Jean's, jeans)

726. Q. What's democratic about nuclear warfare?

A. In nuclear warfare, all men are cremated equal.

727. Judge: State your name and occupation."

Defendant: "My name is Sparks. I'm an electrician."

Judge: "What's the charge?"

Defendant: "I'm charged with battery."

Judge: "Put his man in a dry cell."

728. Two little boys, Tony and Timmy were playing catch in their backyard. They got tired and sat down to rest.

Timmy: "What church do you go to?"

Tony: "I don't know."

Timmy: "Is it Catholic?"

Tony: "No."

Timmy: "Is it Baptist?"

Tony: "No."

Timmy: "Is it Methodist?"

Tony: "No."

Timmy: ""I give up. Don't you really know? Is it Unity?"

Tony: "It's some other abomination."

729.   Q. Did you hear about the man who sat up all night wondering where the sun goes when it went down?

A. It finally dawned on him.

730.   Aggressive boy: "Where can you pick up dates?"

"Angry girl: In the grocery store next to apples."

731.   A young soldier had made a date with a pretty young librarian. He had to break this date because he could not get off duty early enough.

The next afternoon, he went to see the girl at the library. He said to her, "I'm sorry I could not make our date last night. I had to make sure it was All Quiet on the Western Front.

The pretty young librarian did not say a word. She just looked at him.

The young soldier next said, "You're a Midsummer Night's Dream to me."

At this point the young librarian handed the soldier a book. Then she walked away.

The title of the book was: Paradise Lost.

732.   There was an Eskimo who got cold and built a fire in his kayak. The kayak burned up.

Q. What is the moral of this story?

A. You can't have your kayak and heat it too.

(You can't have your cake and eat it too.)

733.   Joe: "I know a man who lost his leg and now has a hickory one."

Moe: "I know a woman who has a cedar chest."

734.   I had a friend who did not know the meaning of <u>fear</u>. He was afraid to ask.

735. Q. What do you call two newly married dandelions?

A. Newly weeds. (newly weds)

736. lst lady: "When I'm down in the dumps, I buy a new hat."

2nd lady: "I always wondered where you got those hats."

737. Q. When is the honeymoon over?

A. The honeymoon is over when she finds out that the man she thought had lots of money and was a big spender was really financially destitute. And it is over when he finds out that his new wife is a big spender.

738. Jane: "I hear your husband's a great gun in industry."

Barb: "Yeah, he's been fired five times."

739. Did you hear about the novelist who got the idea for his second novel from the movie version of his first novel?

740. A well-dressed business man went into a saloon, sat down at the bar, and ordered a beer with an egg in it. A drunk, sitting on the bar stool next to him, asked, "How come you ordered that beer with an egg in it?"

The business man replied, "In the first place, it's none of your business. In the second place, I happen to like eggs, and in the third place, it puts lead in your pencil."

The drunk then ordered the same thing. "I want one of them beers with an egg in it." Shortly, the bartender set the glass down in front of him.

The drunk took one sip, made a face, and slammed the glass down on the bar.

The business man asked, "Why didn't you drink it?"

The drunk replied, "In the first place, it's none of your business. In the second place, I don't like eggs. And in the third place, I ain't got nobody to write to."

(Martha Davis – Conneaut, Ohio, U.S.A.)

741. A man and his wife went into a diner. They began looking at the menu. The husband opened his wallet and found only five dollars. He said to his wife, "What can we get with only five dollars?"

    The waitress, overhearing his question, answered him, "I'd recommend two hamburgers and a three buck tip."

742. Mrs. Lockhorn was busy at her desk, paying the bills. She said to her husband who was reading the newspaper, "I'll handle the bills we <u>can</u> pay. You take care of the others."

743. Epitaph on a tombstone:

    R.I.P. Don't take life too seriously.

    You'll never get out of it alive anyhow.

744. Q. How can you tell the sex of a chromosome?

    A. Pull down its genes. (jeans)

745. A father was having a facts of life talk with his young son. Suddenly the son interrupted and said, "You know, Dad, if you keep telling me about the birds and the bees, I'm gonna lose interest in girls."

746. Biology teacher: "Sometimes a person can't help being fat. It's in his or her genes."

    Bullying student points to a fat student in the class and says, "In his case, it's hanging over his jeans."

747. "We've been happily married for two years – 1975 and 1988."

748. Sally: "How are you children doing in school?"

    Marge: "Well, I still go to PTA meetings under an assumed name."

749.   He is such a good talker that he could talk a dog off a meat truck.

750.   Customer: (to druggist) "Could ou give me a tablet?"

Druggist: "What kind?"

Customer: "A yellow one."

Druggist: "What's wrong with you?"

Customer: "Nothing. I want to write a letter."

751.   He is as honest as a Cardinal's confession.

752.   "If you don't say anything, you won't be called upon to repeat it." (Calvin Coolidge – Silent Cal)

753.   A tightwad was shopping for an inexpensive birthday gift, but the only thing he could find was a badly broken vase. He bought it for almost nothing and asked the store to send it—figuring his friend would think it was broken in the mail.

A week later he received a note: "Many thanks for the vase. It was nice of you to wrap each piece separately."

754.   Q. What has more lives than a cat?

A. A frog. Because it croaks all night.

755.   Small boy: "Grandfather, can you make a sound like a frog?"

Grandfather: "Why should I do that?"

Small boy: "Because Daddy says when you croak, we,ll all be rich."

756.   Q. Why are soldiers tired on April 1st?

A. Because they've just had a thirty-one day march.

757.   Q. Where would you rather be? In a collision or in an explosion?

A. In a collision.

Q. Why?

A. In a collision, there you are. In an explosion, where did everybody go?

758. Joe: "Do you live hear the school?"

Moe: I must be close. When I get home, my mom always says, 'Good grief, are you home already'?"

759. A used car salesman was waxing eloquent about the super buy of a lifetime he was showing a customer. "You can't go wrong with this gem," he proclaimed as he started the engine. It's the opportunity of a lifetime."

"It must be," agreed the customer. "I can hear it knocking."

760. A young boy went to school one day and had a lesson in sex education. When he got home that night, his father asked him, "What did you learn in your sex education class today?"

The young boy thought for a minute, and then he said, "Stay away from intersections. But if you can't stay away from intersections, then buy condominiums."

761. A ramp knocked on the door of a fat lady. When the fat lady answered her door, the tramp said, "I have not eaten for four days."

The fat lady replied, "I wish I had your will power."

762. Joe: "Did you hear about the drunk house?"

Moe: "How could that be?"

Joe: "The owner had his walls plastered."

763. "Nature has given to us one tongue and two ears so that we may hear twice as much as we speak."

(Epictetus -- Greek Philosopher)

764. Q. When do you shop?

A. I shop on the splurge of the moment. (splurge, spur)

765. Knock, knock. Who's there? Banana. Banana who?

Knock, knock. Who's there? Banana. Banana who?

Knock, knock. Who's there? Banana. Banana who?

Knock, knock. Who's there? Orange who?

Orange you glad I did not say banana again? (Aren't you?)

766. An elderly cattle rancher in Wyoming decided to retire.

He asked his three sons to take over the five thousand acre ranch. He also asked them to come up with a new name for the business.

After several days, he asked them, "Have you found a name yet?'

"Yes," said the oldest son who had studied physics in college. "It is FOCUS."

"What does that mean?"

"It's where the sun's rays meet. There's a double meaning.

"It's where the sons raise meat.

767. Q. How do you like bathing beauties?

A. Can't tell. I never bathed any."

768. A mother walked into her so"

The son said, "I don't want to go to school."

"You have to go."

"I hate that school. The kids are mean and rotten."

"You still have to go."

"It's like a jungle. One fight after another. They threaten me a hundred times a day."

"You must go."

"Why must I go?"

"Because you're the principal!" (Milton Berle)

769.   Sign in a bakery window:

OH, WHAT FOOLS THESE MORSLS BE.

770.   Diner (in restaurant): "Waiter, there's a button in my salad."

Waiter: "Oh, it must have come off when the salad was dressing."

771.   Q. Why can't two elephants go into a pool at the same time?

A. Because they only have one pair of trunks.

772.   The following joke dates back to the early days of radio when the ether theory was still in existence. Manly people (including scientists) still believed that the ether was an invisible fluid which permeated all space and made possible the transmission of electromagnetic waves (including radio waves):

Joe: "That radio is making a horrible noise."

Moe: "You would too, if you were coming out of ether."

773.   You can never do something kind for someone too soon, because you never know when too soon can be too late.

774.   Democracy is not a spectator's sport.

775.   The mind is everything. What you think, you become.

776.   The following story is a scene in a vaudeville show in Chicago in 1922. It was told to me by my mother-in-law, Martha Davis, who lived to be one hundred years old:

"The curtain was raised and on the stage were tents, a simulated camp fire, and about fifteen rookies, clad in green fatigues, waiting for mail call.

Soon the mailman arrived, and he handed a large envelope to one of the rookies. The young rooky looked at it and walked to the front of the stage. He said, "This must be from my old landlady, but I've already paid the rent."

Then he opened the envelope and said, "No. It's from my wife." He read the letter aloud: My dear husband. As I have nothing else to do, I shall write you a letter. As I have nothing else to say, I shall close. P.S. The barber has come to our house to stay. The night before last, he took me to a moving picture show, and last night he brought me a pair of silk stockings. He knew the exact size. He is going to stay until you come back. God bless you and keep you – from your loving wife."

777.   Barber: "Well, sonny, how would you like your hair cut?"

Small boy: "If you please, sir, just like my dad's, and don't forget the little round hole at the top where his head comes through"

778.   Joe: "So you are planning to write a real down-to-earth story?"

Moe: "Yeah, it's about a parachute jumper."

779.   Ethan: "I want to do something big and clean."

Tyler: "Then, wash an elephant."

780.   Q. What is the best way to prevent infection caused by biting insects?

A. Don't bite any.

781.   Q. What did the football say to the football player?

A. I get a kick out of you.

782.   Q. What did one math book say to another math book?

A. Don't bother me. I've got my own problems.

783.   A young man applied for a construction job. His future employer asked him, "Can you operate a steam-shovel?"

The young man said, "You can't catch me on that one. Nobody can shovel steam!"

784. A seven-foot tall teenager applied for a job as a lifeguard. The head lifeguard asked him, "Can you swim?"

    The seven-foot tall young man said, "No. But I can sure wade like crazy."

785. Joe: "What happens if you stub your toe in the road?"

    Moe: "You call a tow truck. (toe, tow)

786. Q. Why can't a leopard ever hide?

    A. Because he is always spotted.

787. Q. What kind of lights did Noah use on the Ark?

    A. Floodlights.

788. First moron: "I've got to fix my hourglass. It's been running a little slow."

    Second moron: "It's filled with sand. How can you speed up a sand clock?"

    First moron: "Easy. I'll just put in a little quicksand."

789. The president of the Budweiser Beer Company had a brilliant idea one day. He telephoned the Pope in Rome, Italy, and said, "How about changing one of the lines in the Lord's Prayer? Instead of saying 'Give us this day our daily bread,' say 'Give us this day our Daily Bud.' I'll pay you a secret bonus of $5000 per month. I think of this as an advertising expense."

    The Pope was righteously indignant and slammed down the telephone.

    A week later the President of Budweiser Beer telephoned the Pope again. "How about $10,000 per month?" Again, the Pope slammed down the telephone.

    The president of Budweiser Beer was very persistent. A week later he upped the price to $20,000 per month. Again, the Pope hung up on him

Just about every week the president of Budweiser Beer kept telephoning and upping the price. And the Pope kept hanging up on him.

But the Pope began to do a little thinking and calculating. When the price reached $100,000 per month, the Pope thought to himself, "That's $1,200,000 per year." He neither accepted or rejected the offer. He hung up the phone as usual, but he did not slam it down.

The next day, he called a meeting of his Cardinals. He said to them, "By the way, when does our contract with Pillsbury expire?

(A.A. Silvidi, PhD, Professor of Physics, Kent State Univ.)

790. Teacher: "Where is the Red Sea located?"

Depressed student: "On my report card."

791. Joe: "Did you hear about the woman who got her birth control pills mixed up with her saccharin tablets?

Moe: "No. What happened?"

Joe: "Now she has the sweetest little baby in town."

792. /A young man and a young woman were sitting on a park bench and kissing passionately. When they stopped to come up for air, she said, "And are mine the only lips you have kissed?"

He replied, "Yes, and they are the sweetest of all."

793. Scott: If you are alone in a bar and a mad lion and a mad bull are in this room with you, and you have a gun with only one bullet in it, which would you shoot first? The mad lion or the mad bull?"

Kevin: "I'd shoot the mad bull."

Scott: "No, you should shoot the mad lion."

Kevin: "Why the lion and not the bull?"

Scott: "Because you can shoot the bull anytime."

794. Two convicts were walking down the hallway of a state penitentiary one day. The governor of the state was also walking down this hall and toward them.

One of the convicts bumped into the governor. "Oh, pardon me, sir," said the embarrassed convict."

"Certainly," said the governor and he smiled..

After the two convicts walked on, one convict said to the other, "You should have gotten that in writing."

795. A man's wife was named Kate. His mistress was named Edith. When his wife found out about his mistress, she said, "You can't have your Kate and Edith, too."

(You can't have your cake and eat it, too.)

796. Q. What do you call a scared flower arranger?

A. A petrified florist.

797. A farmer and his wife went to the state fair and saw all the new airplanes. The farmer was fascinated.

"How much for a ride?" asked the farmer.

"Twenty bucks for ten minutes," said the pilot. The farmer and his wife turned to walk away.

"Tell ya what I'll do," said he pilot. "If you don't say a word while we're in the air, I'll take you up for free. But one word and it's $20.

So they went up and flew around for ten minutes, and when they landed, the pilot said, "Congratulations, you made it. Your ride is free!"

"Yeah," the farmer said. "But I almost yelled when my wife fell out."

798. Sunday School Teacher: "Johnny, would you like to go to Heaven?"

   Johnny: "Yes, but Mom told me to come right home after Sunday school."

799. Question on test: Why does the sun never set on the British flag?

   Student's answer: Because they take it in at night.

800. Q. Why is a dog biting his tail like a good manager?

   A. Because he makes both ends meet.

801. Q. What is a monastery?

   A. A home for unwed fathers.

802. Q. If, at first, you don't succeed, what should you do next?

   A. Read the directions.

803. Forgive your enemies, but never forget their names.

804. 1st, guy: "Why do you always win at cards but always lose at horse races?"

   2nd guy: "That's because I can't keep a horse up my sleeve."

805. Q. When do we finally find happiness?

   A. Happiness comes when we stop wailing about the troubles we have and give thanks for the troubles we don't have.

806. A son says to his dad: "I'm going out tonight. I'm looking for a good time—wine, women, and song. Don't try to stop me."

   Dad: "Who's trying to stop you, son? I'm going with you."

807. "Everything is funny as long as it is happening to somebody else." (Will Rogers)

808. Psychiatrist: "What is your problem?"

Man patient: "I try to make my life exciting, but my wife always finds out about it."

809. The race to get Dad a Christmas present often ends in a tie.

810. Daisy: "Tom, darling, you would be a marvelous dance if it were _not_ for two things."

Tom: "What are they?"

Daisy: "Your feet."

811. When it comes to giving, some people stop at nothing.

812. Q. What do you call two convicts who become buddies in jail?

A. Pen Pals (Pen—slang for penitentiary)

813. Q. What do you say wen a robber is headed for your bakery?

A. Quick. Hide all the dough.

814. Q. What do you get when you cross a pig and a pine tree?

A. A porky pine. (porcupine)

815. Q. What did the boy octopus say to the girl octopus?

A. I want to hold your hand, hand, hand, hand, hand, hand, hand, hand.

816. Joe: "What do you mean by saying that you come from a broken home?"

Moe: "I've got a crack in my basement wall."

817. A young man said to a young lady clerk in a men's clothing store, "Could I try on that suit in the window?"

The young lady smiled and said, "I'd rather have you go and use the dressing room."

818. Q. What is found in a mailbox, has no arms and legs, but has a man's name?

A. Bill

819. During a geology lecture the professor said, "The earth will probably end in five billion yeas."

    A hand went up in the back of the classroom, and a voice anxiously asked, "Did you say five <u>million</u> years?"

    "No," the professor said, "five <u>billion.</u>"

    "Oh, that's better," the voice answered with a sigh of relief.

820. The preacher asked, "How many animals of each species did Moses take with him in the arc?"

    Several hands went up, and the people said, "two" simultaneously.

    "No, that's wrong. None is the answer. It was <u>Noah</u>, not Moses who had he arc."

821. An eager beaver young reporter directed a particularly complex question to an old politician.

    The old politician smiled and replied, "I wish I had an answer to that question, because I'm tired of answering that question."

822. What are the seven ages of man? \

    Twenty is when you want to wake up romantic.

    Thirty is when you want to wake up married.

    Forty is when you want to wake up successful.

    Fifty is when you want to wake up rich.

    Sixty is when you want to wakeup contented.

    Seventy is when you want to wake up healthy.

    Eighty is when you <u>just</u> want to wake up.

823. Dad: "How did you do on your history test?"

    Son: Not so well. They asked me about things that happened before I was born.

824. Son: "will you help me with my math problems?

Dad: "That wouldn't be right."

Son: "They aren't right when I do them either."

825. Ethan: "What do masochism and amnesia mean?"

Tyler: "Beats me. I forget."

826. Patient: "Doctor, you have to help me. I just can't remember anything anymore."

Doctor: "How long have you had his?"

Patient: "Had what?"

827. Tom: "Whenever she calls me, she calls me handsome."

Mack: "Why does she call you handsome when she needs money?

Tom. "She says <u>hand some</u> over."

828. He was old and had an ugly face. He said to the woman to whom he had just proposed, "You are the sixth woman to whom I have proposed without avail."

"Well," said the woman, "Maybe if you wear one (a veil) when making your seventh proposal, you'll have better luck."

829. The bee is such a busy soul / He has no time for birth control. / And that is why in times like these / There are so many sons of bees.

830. Three old men were riding on a bus. The windows were wide open. One of them said, "It's windy today, isn't it?"

The second one said, ""No, it's not Wednesday, it's Thursday."

Third one said, ""Yes, I'm thirsty, too, let's all get off and have a drink."

831. A man's home is now his hassle.

832.   It's better to have loved short girl than never to have loved <u>a</u> <u>tall</u>. (at all)

833.   "I used to walk a lot," said the gym major. But it gave me big feet. Then, I learned to swim, but that gave me big arms."

   Her so-called 'good friend' then said, "You also tried horseback riding, didn't you. And what did that give you?"

834.   1ˢᵗ lady: "My husband and I attend to our budget every evening. It's more economical that way. We save money."

   2ⁿᵈ lady: "Why is that?"

   1ˢᵗ lady: "By the time we get it balanced, it is too late to go anywhere."

835.   On a house constructing job, two morons were hammering nails into 2" x 4" studs. The first moron held up a nail, then threw it away. He held up another nail and threw it away. The third nail he picked up, he hammered it into the stud.

   The second moron asked, "How come you threw away the first two nails?"

   The first moron replied, "Because the heads are on the wrong side."

836.   Two hot air balloons were gliding very low over the desert. Said one to the other, "Watch out for that cactussssssss!"

837.   Mary: "What are your daughters' names?"

   Jane: "Rose, Pansy, Daisy, Petunia,and Artificial?"

   Mary: "Why the last name – Artificial?"

   Jane: "I couldn't think of any other flowers."

838.   In a barbershop a manicurist was giving a man a manicure. The following dialogue occurred:

   He: "How about a date tonight?"

She: "I'm married."

He: "Well, call your husband and tell him you are spending the night at a girlfriend's house."

She: "Tell him yourself. My husband is shaving you right now."

839.	Rose and Daisy, two office workers, were describing their Saturday night dates.

Rose: I had to slap his face five times!"

Daisy: "Was he fresh?"

Rose: "No, I thought he was dead."

840.	Joe: "Those flies are pesky. Don't you ever shu them?"

Moe: "No, they like going around bare foot."

841.	Q. What is the key to a young man's success?

A. The one that fits he ignition.

842.	Customer: "I want a mustard plaster."

Clerk: "We're out of mustard? How about mayonnaise?"

843.	Customer: "Did you fix the brakes on my car?"

Mechanic: "I couldn't fix our brakes, so I made your horn louder."

844.	A man sitting at a lunch counter in a diner saw a pie behind the counter that looked delicious.

He said to the waitress, "For dessert, I'd like a piece of that raisin pie back there." He pointed toward the pie.

The waitress began to pick up the pie, but stopped and waved her hands. She said, "Shoo fly, shoo fly. Turning to the man, she said, "Sir, that ain't a raisin pie. That's an apple pie."

845.	Our life is what our thoughts make it.

846. Mrs. Jones: "Don't let our dog into my house. It's full of fleas. Mrs. Smith: "I never dreamed you'd let your house get into that condition?"

847. A man fell off a cliff. On the way down, he caught hold of a tree root. As he was hanging in midair, he cried to heaven, "Is anyone out there?"

    A disembodied voice answered, "Yes, my son. Let go and I will bear thee up."

    The man hesitated. Then he cried out, "Anyone else?"

848. Q. How can you prevent acid rain?

    A. By seeding clouds with Roll Aids.

849. Madison: "I understand she was very aggressive. She threw herself at him, so to speak."

    Caitlyn: "Yes. That's true. They met in an automobile accident."

850. A nun, wearing her habit of white and black, was playing golf with one of her male friends. Her male friend happened to be fond of swearing.

    After swinging at the ball sitting on the tee, he said, "God damn it, I missed!"

    "Oh, please don't swear," the nun said.

    They continued playing. About ten minutes later, and after swinging at the ball sitting on the tee, he said, "Damn it, I missed again!"

    "Oh, please don't swear. God hears everything you say. He may come down and do something errible."

    The sky began to darken, but they want ed to finish their game before the rain.

    Her male friend said again, ""Damn it, I missed.!"

The nun was very indigent. "If you do that one more time, God will get even with you. He'll send a bolt of lightning down here and strike you dead."

After three minutes, the man said again, "Damn it, I missed!"

Just then a white bolt of lightning came down and struck the nun. <u>She lay dead on the ground.</u>

Then a loud disembodied voice came booming down from the heavens: <u>"Damn it, I missed!</u>

851. Joe: "Did you hear that in Alaska some Eskimos still use fish for money?"

Moe: "That must really messup he vending machines."

852. Pizza Man: "Do you want me to cut your pizza into eight pieces or six pieces?"

Customer: "You better make it six. I don't think I can ear eight?"

853. In describing his poverty stricken childhood, a man said,

"My folks were so poor that we couldn't even keep up with the neighbors, and they were on welfare.

854. Two young children had just left a sex education class.

Here is their conversation:

Ethan: "I'm not saying I don't believe it."

Ryan: "Isn't that the way it happens?"

Ethan: "I'm not saying I don't believe it. I'm just saying that they should give equal time to the stork theory."

855. Q. What is the difference between men and women?

A. There is a VAS DIFFERENS between men and women.

856. Judge: "Why did you steal that car?"

Crook: "I saw it parked outside a cemetery, so I thought the owner didn't need it anymore."

857.　Doctor: "I can't do anything about your problem. It's hereditary."

Patient: "Good. Send the bill to my father."

858.　Q. Where do you go if you want to go to a school that will give you a sense of direction?

A. Go east and attend West Point.

859.　A young man was making a confession to his priest. The priest told him, "Young man, you're not making a confession. You are bragging."

860.　The gas man went to a house and rang the bell. When the lady of the house answered the door, the gas man said, "I understand something is not working."

The lady of the house replied, "Yeah, he's upstairs."

861.　A small boy had lost several of his baby teeth. He said, "If I lose any more teeth, I'll be running on my rims."

862.　A Catholic priest and a Jewish Rabbi were seated next to one another in an airplane. They were visiting, but from time t to Catholicism.

Then the plane crashed. Everyone survived. The Catholic priest was in one corner of he fuselage and he Jewish rabbi was in the other. The Catholic priest observed that the Jewish Rabbi was crossing himself in the traditional Catholic manner. He put his fingers to his forehead, then to each side of his body, and so forth.. So the Catholic priest said to the Jewish Rabbi, "I see that I've finally got you converted to the Catholic faith. You're crossing yourself."

The Jewish Rabbi replied, "No, I'm not crossing myself. I'm just checking."

"What are you checking," the Catholic priest asked."

The Jewish Rabbi replied, "Spectacles, testicles, wallet, and watch."

863. A young lady heard that a milk bath was good for her health. She said to her milkman, "Could I have ten gallons of milk?"

The milkman asked her, "Do you want it pasteurized?"

The lady exclaimed, "Oh, No. Just up to my thighs."

(past your eyes)

864. She. "Did you eve hear about lover's leap?"

He: "That's the distance from one bed to another."

865. Teacher: "Who lived in ancient Egypt?"

Student: "Ancient Egypt was mostly inhabited by mummies."

866. Q. There were five people under one umbrella. Why didn't they get wet?

A. Because it wasn't raining.

867. A traveling salesman was having a wild week-end with his mistress in the big city. His conscience was bothering him so he sent a postcard to his wife in his hometown. He inadvertently wrote: "Having a wonderful time. Wish you were _her_."

868. They were married and lived happily <u>even</u> after.

869. Patient: "What should I do if I have ringing in my ears?"

Doctor: "Don't answer."

870. Q. What is a diagnosis?

A. What a sick person must make before he can determine what specialist to call.

871. Philosophy professor: "Miss Jones, can you tell the class the name of the philosopher who wrote *The Critique of Pure Reason?*"

Miss Jones (embarrassed and blushing): "I can't!"

Philosophy professor: "Good! That's the first correct answer you've given all year!" (Immanuel Kant)

872. A man took his second-hand car to a garage for service. He said, "Please change the oil."

The mechanic told him, "You should keep the oil and change the car.

873. Q. Instead of writing "Sincerely yours", "Yours truly,"etc., what does an undertaker write?

A. "Eventually yours"

874. Q. Why is the funeral business so profitable?

A. Because people are just dying to get in.

875. A man and wife had been married for many years. The wife contracted a terminal illness.

She said to her husband, "After I am dead, I want you to marry again." And I want your new wife to be as happy as I have been. I want you to give her my things. Will you give her my perls?"

"Yes," her husband said.

"Will you give her my mink coat?"

"Yes," her husband said.

"Will you give her my golf clubs?"

"No," her husband said.

"Why not?"

"Because she's left handed," her husband said.

876. At 20, a girl will ask, "Is he good looking?"

At 30, she asks, "Is he rich?"

At 35, she asks, "Where is he?"

877.   Many people could learn from their mistakes if they were not so busy denying that they made them.

878.   Q. Why should we all be concerned about the future?

A. Because we have to spend the rest of our lives there.

879.   Q. What is the daffynition of fat?

A. Energy gone to waist. (waste)

880.   Joe: "Did you say you were a light eater?"

Moe: "Absolutely."

Joe: "But, man, you must weigh over 250 pounds."

Moe: "270 pounds."

Joe: "And you say you're a light eater?"

Moe: Absolutely. As soon as it's light, I start eating."

881.   A young woman was having morning sickness, so she went to see her doctor. After a thorough examination, he said to her, "You're pregnant. Break the news to your husband."

"I don't have a husband," said the young woman.

"Then, tell your boyfriend."

"I don't have a boyfriend."

"Tell the guys you've slept with."

The young woman was indignant and felt insulted. She protested, "I haven't slept with any guys!"

Then the doctor said, "You'd better tell your mother to get ready for the second coming of Christ. This is gonna be a virgin birth."

882.   Son: "Dad, how can these rock groups afford all their expensive instruments?"

Dad. "Think of all the money they have saved on music lessons."

883.   Q. When two cars are lined up head to tail, waiting for a red light to change to green, which car will see the change first?"

A. The second car back. He always honks his horn.

884.   Yesterday is a canceled check.

Tomorrow is a promissory note.

Today is ready cash. Use it wisely.

885.   Q. What do you call a cow that eats grass?

A. A lawn moo-er.

886.   Q. What long word usually has only one letter in it

A. An envelope.

887.   A vacuum cleaner salesman was assigned a territory by his boss. His boss told him, "At the end of each day, I want you to send me a telegram and let me know how you have done."

At the end of the first day, the salesman sent telegram which read: "No sales. Good contacts. It's a feather in my cap."

The second day was much like the first. The salesman was friendly and persuasive, bu there were no sales. He sent a similar telegram to his boss: "Still no sales. Good contacts. It's a feather in my cap."

The same thing continued for eight more days. At the end of each day, the telegram read: "No sales. Good contacts. It's a feather in my cap."

On the next day the salesman realized he was out of money, so he sent a telegram o his boss: "Out of cash. Send money so I can take the train home."

His boss sent him a telegram which read: "Stick those ten feathers in your hind end and fly home."

(Martha Davis – Conneaut, Ohio)

888. Abstinence is a good thing. It should always be practiced in moderation.

889. A young Eskimo man had just proposed to his girlfriend. The girlfriend was not interested.

    The young man exclaimed, "What do you have to say to me when I've driven over 100 miles to come and say, "I love you and I want you to be my wife?"

    The girl replied calmly, "I'd say that's a lot of mush."

890. Blessed is the man who can laugh at himself for he can always be amused.

891. A man went to a ritzy hotel for a change and a rest. The bellboys got the change and the hotel got the rest.

892. A soldier went to Las Vegas for a change and a rest. The maids got the change and the blackjack dealers got the rest.

893. Q. They say that a man with a green thumb is a good gardener. But what do you call a man with a purple thumb?

    A. A do-it-yourself carpenter.

894. Patient: "I can't remember in which block my house is."

    Doctor: "Don't worry. It must be a mental block."

895. A husband who was newly retired was weary of sitting around the house. He needed a hobby. He said to his wife, "Maybe I should take up painting."

    His wife said, "You can start with the kitchen."

896. A Sunday school teacher was trying to teach her pupils the difference between right and wrong. She asked. "Is stealing right or wrong?" Then she had a brainstorm and said, "Suppose a woman finds a man's wallet on the dresser and she sees that

he is sound asleep. She decides to open it and takes out fifty dollars. Is that right or wrong?"

A little girl raised her hand.

"Yes, Mary," she said.

"That would be his wife," Mary said.

The Sunday school teacher was nonplussed. She felt as though the little girl had thrown a monkey wrench into her wheels. She did know what to say. Thankfully, the bell rang and the children rushed out

897.   Q. What were the famous last words of Eli Whitney?

A. Keep your cotton picking fingers off my gin.

898.   Wife: "That was a terrible thunder and lightning sorm last night. How could you sleep?"

Husband: "Well, why did you wake me up so I'd know about it?"

899.   My wife never lies about her age. She just tells everyone she is as old as I am, and hen lies about my age.

900.   The highway patrolman stopped a speeding motorist on I-71. The speed limit was 55 miles per hour.

The patrolman asked the lady motorist, "Do you know what he speed limit is?"

"Yes, it's 71," the lady replied.

The patrolman exclaimed, "Well, it's a good thing I stopped you before you got onto I-480."

901.   A housewife telephoned a refrigerator repairman. After he finished fixing her refrigerator, he said he charge would be eighty dollars.

The housewife replied angrily, "That's ridiculous. You only worked for one minute. I demand to have an itemized bill."

So the repairman w rote on a piece of paper:

Turning a screw..........$2.00

Knowing where to turn the screw........$78.00

Total $80.00

902. A farm boy and a city girl were courting. They were out in the pasture watching two cows nuzzle one another.

The farm boy said, "Gee, I'd like to do that."

The city girl replied, "Go ahead. It's your cow."

903. "When I was younger I could remember everything—whether it happened or not."…"I remember it perfectly—whether it happened or not." (Mark Twain)

904. "Too much of a good thing is a good thing. Too much of a good thing is wonderful." (Mae West)

905. Q. What kind of a dog wears a sweater?

A. A Chile dog.

906. Joe: "Wasn't that a bad drought we had?"

Moe: "Yes, it was so dry the cows were giving powdered milk."

907. If idle chatter could be bought and sold, we'd all be rich.

908. Patient: "My problem is, I have a suicidal complex."

Doctor: "In that case, you'll have to pay in advance."

909. A pig and a hen were discussing a ham and egg breakfast. The hen said, "Why don't you want to go the ham and egg breakfast?"

The pig replied, "For you, it is a donation. For me, it is a commitment."

910. Teacher: "What is a Laplander?"

Student: "That is a person who loses his balance on a bus."

911. Customer: "I'd like to buy an engagement ring. About one hundred and fifty dollars."

     Saleslady: While binging out a tray, she said, "This is our Can-Hardly brand."

     Customer: "What does that mean?"

     Saleslady: "Can hardly see 'em."

912. Q. Why did he moron put on a wet shirt?"

     A. The label said: WASH and WEAR.

913. Never let yesterday use up today.

914. A barber said o a customer, "Your hair needs cutting badly."

     The customer said, "No, my hair needs cutting nicely. You cut it badly last time."

915. Q. What did old McDonald see when he took the eye test?"

     A. E I E I O

916. Scott: "Why are you making faces at my bull dog?"

     Kevin: "He started it."

917. A teacher was telling a friend about one of her students. "He cheats, he lies, he steals, he hits, and to make it even worse, he's the only one in the class with a perfect attendance record." (Milton Berle)

918. Once there was a man who took a vacation to forget everything. In his hotel room he opened his suitcase and found that he'd forgotten everything. (Milton Berle)

919. Q. What smells like hell, has four wheels, and flies?

     A. A garbage truck. (Milton Berle)

920. Q. What did Mama Lightning Bug say to Papa Lightning Bug?

     A. Isn't Junior bright for his age?

921.   Q. What do you call two convicts who become buddies in jail?

A. Pen Pals.

922.   Q Why do chickens go to a museum?

A. To see an eggsibit. (exibit)

923.   Joe: "How do you catch a wild rabbit?"

Moe: "You sneak up on him."

Joe: "Well, then, how do you catch a tame rabbit?"

Moe: "The tame way." (same)

924.   Mother: "At open house, your teacher told me there were five questions on your last test. Did you miss any?"

Son: "Only the first three and the last two."

925.   1st Moron: "I lost my dog."

2nd Moron: "Why don't you put an ad in the paper?"

1st Moron: "My dog can't read."

926.   She: "What do you do after you finish playing post office?"

He: "Play pony express."

She: "What's that?"

He: "There's more horsing around?

927.   A young man asked the middle-age lady bartender, "Where can you pick up dates?"

She replied, pretending to be insulted, "At the supermarket next to the raisins."

928.   He: "Will you marry me and spend he rest of your life with me?

She: "No."

He: "How about weekends?"

929. Bumper Sticker: IF YOU CAN READ THIS, YOU'RE TOO DAMN CLOSE.

930. A young man took his girlfriend in his arms. "Oh, darling," he murmured. "I love you so. Please say you will be mine. I'm not rich like Charlie Ross. I haven't a Cadillac or a mansion or a swimming pool. But, darling, I do love you, and I can't live without you."

    Two soft arms stole around his neck, and two ruby-red lips whispered in his ear, Where is this man, Charlie Ross?"

931. A man was in the IRS office. He was being audited. After the IRS officer completed his work, he said, "I'll call you a cab."

    "Oh, don' bother," the man who was being audited replied, "I've got my car parked right outside."

    The IRS officer then glared at him and said, "What car!"

932. Deep in the night, a man shook his wife, "Joyce, wake up."

    His wife said, "What's the matter?"

    "Darling," he said, "I got you two aspirins and a glass of water."

    Joyce sat up. "What's this for?" she asked.

    "For your headache, darling."

    "Who has a headache?" she asked.

    "You don't have a headache?"

    "No," she answered.

    "Great. Let's make love."

933. Epitaph on an early American tombstone:

    "Here lies a man who looked into the barrel of his gun to see if it was loaded. It was."

934. Another epitaph:

"It wasn't a cough that carried him off.

It was a coffin they carried him off in."

935. Man: "I'd like to marry you, but I am penniless."

Woman: "That's nothing. The Czar of Russia was Nicholas." (nickel less)

936. Ethan: "Did you hear that Joe's Pizza Store was closed down?"

Tyler: "Yeah. They were masking their own dough!"

Ethan: "So what's wrong with a pizza place making their own dough?"

Tyler: "Twenty dollar bills!"

937. Q. What did Mrs. Bullet say to Mr. Bullet?

A. We're going to have a BB/

938. A small boy stood on the bathroom scales. He said to his father who was shaving at the sink, "Hey Dad! This thing does not hurt me at all."

His dad asked, "Why should it hurt you?"

His son answered, "Mom groans every time she gets on this thing."

939. Jane: "Did Joe propose?"

Joan: "Yes, but I turned him down on account of the book I was reading."

Jane: "What could your reading a book have to do with refusing him?"

Joan: "Well, my sister's husband proposed to her while she was reading *The Three Musketeers,* and she had triplets."

Jane: "So?"

Joan: "When Joe proposed, I was reading *Birth of a Nation.*"

940.   A man came home from church with two black eyes. His wife asked, "What happened?"

He explained, "Well, when we stood up to sing, I noticed that the lady in front of me had a dress that was stuffed into her underpants. I figured I'd do her a favor and pull it out. So I did. She turned around, slammed me with her purse and gave me a black eye."

"Well, then, how did you get the other black eye?" asked his wife.

"Well, I figured I'd better put the dress back into her underpants. I did so. Then she slammed my other eye."

(Martha Davis, Conneaut, Ohio)

941.   Q. Why does a golfer wear two pairs of pants?

A. That's in case he gets a hole in one.

942.   Daddy came home from the office with a brief case full of papers.

Junior, who was six years old and a first grader, asked his mother, "Why?"

His mother explained, "Daddy can't get all his work done at the office."

Junior then said, "Why don't they just put him in a slow group?"

A Student's Prayer

Now I lay me down to study.

I pray the Lord I won't go nutty.

If I should die before I learn this junk,

I pray the Lord that I won't flunk.

If any of me is left at all,

Take my bones to study hall.

943.   Q. What did the egg in the monastery say?

A. Tough luck! It's out of the frying pan and into the friar. (fire)

944.   Q. What do the COLORS have to do with human behavior?"

A. If you lose your temper, you see RED.

If you have a good day, it's a RED letter day.

If you are envious of someone, you are GREEN with envy.

If you are inexperienced, you are GREEN as grass or a GREEN horn.

If you are sad, you feel BLUE.

If you do something once in a while, you do it once in a BLUE moon.

If you are a coward, you are YELLOW.

If you are sick, you might be WHITE as a sheet.

945.   Q. What is the daffynition of football?

A. A game in which one side of the stadium wants to see eleven men killed. Also, it is a game in which the other side of the stadium wants to see eleven men killed.

946.   Q. Why is Thanksgiving called a stuffing time?

A. First you stuff your turkey.

Then you stuff yourself.

Then you stuff your refrigerator with left-overs.

Then you stuff yourself into your clothes.

947.   A 95 year old man went to see his doctor. After the doctor examined the old man, the doctor said, "You've got some

health problems. You are going to have to give up one half of your sex life."

The old man replied, "Which half, Doctor? Talking about it, or thinking about it?"

948. Always do what is right. It will gratify some people and astonish the rest. (Mark Twain)

949. Learn from the mistakes of others. You may not live long enough if you make them all yourself.

950. Half the world is filled up with people who have something to say and can't. And the other half is filled up with people who have nothing to say and won't stop. (Robert Frost)

951. Doctor: "Why haven't you been following my directions and taking your medicine?"

Patient: "I have been, Doctor. It says 'Keep the bottle tightly closed at all times.'"

952. Professor: "Please use the word horticulture in a sentence."

Class clown: "You can lead a whore to culture, but you can't make her think." (Bob Maxwell, SanFrancisco)

953. Preacher's motto: Work for the Lord. The pay is not much, but the rewards are out of this world

954. A telephone solicitor dialed a number. From his list, he knew the number belonged to a Mr. Jones. Assuming a cheerful tone, he said, "How are you today, Mr. Jones?"

Mr. Jones angrily replied, "Terrible! I'm sick! My car's broken! My roof's leaking! I need a vacation!. And I hate telephone solicitors!"

The telephone solicitor cheerfully answered, "Then you need a subscription to our monthly magazine—*1001 Jokes and Belly Laughs.*

955. A country woman went into town to see if she could get a loan to build a bathroom in her house. Since she had never been in a bank before, she was nervous. She got right to the point with the bank president. She said, I want to borrow a thousand dollars to put a bathroom in my house."

The bank president was cautious and replied, "I don't believe I know you. Where have you done your business before?"

"Oh -- out back in the outhouse," the country woman replied."

956. When you're young, your security is your youth. When you're old, you'd damn better well have money.

In God we trust. All others pay cash.

957. Prosperity makes many friends. Adversity trusts them.

958. School is a building with four walls and tomorrow inside.

959. If you realize today that you are not as wise as you thought you were yesterday, you're wiser today.

960. Three Army veterans met after a long separation. Over a table in the cafeteria they were reminiscing in low voices, recalling various unsavory evens in their Army careers, and enjoying themselves immensely. All was ruined, however, when an elderly woman of most proper appearance murmured an apology – "It's very crowded." – and took the fourth seat. The three men found themselves reduced to speechlessness and glowered at the old prim lady, who ignoring them, ate slowly, steadily, and calmly.

Clearly, they would have to maneuver her into leaving.

One of the suddenly had an idea. Winking at the others, he said, "Fellows, I was at a wedding last week. My old man finally married my old lady."

The second man caught on and said, "That's a coincidence. My father is planning a June wedding with my mother next year. I'm the only kid, as it seems, so why don't you two guys join me and make it more fun?"

The third man heaved a sigh. "You guys are lucky. I don't think my dad is ever going to marry Mumsy."

With that, all three men cast sidewise glances at the old lady who spoke loudly, "Will one of you three bastards pass the salt, please?" She smiled nicely, sprinkled salt on her food, and continued eating.

961.   Q. Why is falling in love at first sight a good thing?

     A. It saves time.

962.   Q. If you spend your vacation in your own backyard, what will your friends and neighbors think?"

     A. They will know that you are sensitive, introspective, home-loving, and BROKE.

963.   If you tried to do something and failed, you are better off than if you had ried to do nothing and succeeded.

964.   Teacher: "What is the connecting link between the animal and vegetable kingdoms?"

     Class clown: "Hash."

965.   Teacher: "How do you define ignorance?"

     Student: "It's when you don't know something and somebody else finds it out."

966.   Riddles: WHAT STATE AM I IN?

     Q. I am often found hanging on a line. What state am I in?

     A. Wash. (Washington)

     Q. I am not feeling well. What state am I in?

     A. Ill. (Illinois)

     Q. You're you. What st ate are you in?

A. Me. (Maryland)

Q. You ae a father. What state are ou in?

A. Pa. (Pennsulvania)

967.   The race to get Dad a Christmas present often ends in a tie.

968.   The following are some church bulletin announcements which should have never seen the light of day:

This afternoon there will be a meeting in the south and north sides of the church. Children will be baptized at both ends.

The service will end with "Little Drops of Water." One of the ladies will start qietly and the rest of the congregation will join in.

On Sunday, a special collection will be taken to defray the expenses of the new carpet. All those wishing to do something on the carpet please come forward and get a piece of paper.

The ladies of the church have cast off clothing of every kind, and they may be seen in the church basement on Friday afternoon.

Thursday at 5:00 p.m. there will be a meeting of the Little Mothers club. All wishing to become little mothers will please meet the minister in his study.

Wednesday, the Ladies Literary society will meet. Ms. Johnson will sing "Put Me in My Little bed," accompanied by the peacher.

969.   She: "Why are you wearing a toothbrush in your coat lapel?"

He: "It's my class pin. I go to Colgate."

970.   A young man said to his fiancée, "Honey, I'd go through fire and water for you."

She replied, "Okay make I fire. I'd rat her have you hot than all wet."

971.   A wife confided to her maid. "My husband has been dating his secetary."

The maid replied, "I don't believe a wod of it. You're only trying to make me jealous."

972.   One politician said to a fellow politician, "I certainly admire the straight forward way you dodged all he issues."

973.   A newspaper reporter directed his question to a silver-tongue politician. The politician hastily replied, "I wish I had answer to that question, because I'm tired of answering that question."

"When a thing is funny, search it for a hidden truth."

–George Bernard Shaw—

974.   An efficiency expert was discussing his findings with the office manager. The efficiency expert said, "The workers in this office need a regular program of physical exercise."

The office manager replied, "No one in this office needs any physical exercise. They're getting plenty."

"How so?"

The office manager continued, "They are always flying off the handle, dodging responsibility, climbing the ladder of success, running off at the mouth, stretching the truth, and pushing their luck."

975.   A woman gave birth to twin girls in a hospital. This woman didn't have much formal education, having completed only the eighth grade, and she was ignorant about many common things.

As she lay in her hospital bed recuperating, she began to wonderabout what names to call her twins. On the table next to her bed was a small medical booklet filled with medical vocabulary, of course.

In her mind, she viewed this as a "doctor book." She began looking at the words. At last she found wo words which she liked. She fancied she knew how to pronounce them.

Later in the day, the doctor came to visit. "Well," he said, "Have you decided what names to call your twin girls?"

"Yes," she answered. "Sifil' is." (accent after the l') is one name I like."

"And what is the other?" asked the doctor.

"Gonor'ra" (accent after the first r)

By this time the doctor could not help himself. He howled with laughter, put his hand over his mouth and quickly left the room. [syphilis, gonorrhea]

(This is a true story told to the author by a hospital nurse.)

976.   Q. What do you call a herd of rabbits hopping backwards?

A. A receding hair line. (hare line)

977.   Teacher: Where is your homework?

Student: My dog ate it.

Teacher: You know, your brother Mike used that same excuse on me years ago.

Student: Well, it's the same dog, too.

978.   A secretary in a big office finally got engaged to the office playboy. He gave her a ring.

The next day the secretary wore the ring to the office. That evening her mother said, "I'll bet you got some raves about your ring."

"Yes, I did. In fact, some of the girls recognized it."

979.   Q. What happens if a glass blower breathes in?

A. He'd end up with a pain in his lungs.

980.   One's character is made up of what he or she does when no one is looking.

981.   A man opened his front door and said to his wife, "Do you realize I just drove my Japanese car to a Japanese owned video store for a Japanese distributed film to play in our Japanese VCR on our Japanese TV?"

His wife asked, "What film did you get?"

He replied, "Thirty Seconds Over Tokyo."

982.   An old maid had a dog named snoopy. Shealso had a jr with a genie in it. One day she said o he genie in the bottle, "Come on out."

The genie came out of the bottle and asked, "What can I do for you? I can grant you one wish."

The old maid said, "I don't have a boyfriend. Could you turn my dog Snoopy into a beautiful handsome young man? I need a lover."

The genie performed his magic, and the dog turned into a handsome young man.

The old maid said to the young man, "Now, make love to me."

The young man said, "I can't."

The old maid said, "Why can't you? Weren't you my do Snoopy and now you are a handsome virile young man?"

The young man said, "Don't you remember? You had me fixed."

983.   Q. Why did the potato cross the road?

A. He saw a fork up ahead.

984. Joe: Is your house warm?

     Moe: It should be. The painters gave it three coats of paint last week?

985. Q. How did McDonald's celebrate his engagement with Wendy's?

     A. With an onion ring.

986. Q. Why did Junior Rock run away from the quarry?

     A. He was tired of being taken for granite. (granted)

987. Q. Why did the two old coin collectors meet for dinner?

     A. For old dimes' sake.

988. Q. Why did the kangaroo see he family psychiatrist?

     A. He was feeling a little jumpy.

989. Jack: Did you hear about the young married couple who did not know the difference between Vaseline and putty:?

     Mack: No, what happened?

     Jack: All their windows fell out.

990. An old man and an old woman went to bed early every night. They would hold hands for about five minutes and then roll over and go to sleep. Nothing else happened. This was the extent of their love making.

     One night, the old man reached out for his wife's hand, but the wife pulled her hand away. The old man asked, "What's the matter?"

     The old wife replied, "Not tonight, darling. I've got a headache."

991. Joe: "I've eaten a lot of beef all my life, and I am as strong as an ox."

     Moe: "That's strange. I've eaten fish all my life, but I can't swim a stroke."

992. Judge (to prisoner). "I thought I told you last time that I did not want to see you here again."

     Prisoner: That's what I told the policeman, but he did not believe me."

993. There was a rich cattle baron who lived in sunny sunny Arizona. He was on his death bed. He called all his sons to his death bed and whispered, "I want all you boys to carry on and raise the finest cattle, and I want you to call the ranch FOCUS."

     The oldest son asked, "Why should we call the ranch FOCUS?"

     The dying father's last wods were, "FOCUS, because that's where the sons raise meat." (sun's rays meet)

994. Patient: "I have terrible nightmares. A big monster is always chasing me. Just as he is about to catch me, the alarm goes off and I escape. What should I do?

     Doctor: "Never forget to set our alarm."

995. Q. Why should a man hold his girl friend's hand while they are in a theatre watching a movie?

     A. To prevent her from eating all the popcorn.

996. Q. What is a raving beauty?

     A. Definition of a girl who comes in second place in a beauty conest.

997. Q. How do make the number One disappear?

     A. Put a letter G in front of it, and it's GONE.

998. Q. What goes around the world while staying in one place? A a stamp.

999. A man is incomplete until he gets married, and then he's finished.(Ga Ga Gabor)

1000. Father: "How did you do in school today?"

Son: "I'm like George Washington?"

Father: "How's that?"

Son: "I went down in history."

1001. 1ˢᵗ kid: "My father has George Washington's watch. It's been handed down in the family."

2ⁿᵈ kid: "That's nothing. My father has Adam's apple."

1002. A motorist stopped at a roadside restaurant called SARAH'S HOME COOKING. He ordered a meal and began eating. He called the waiter to his table. He said, This is terrible. Where is Sarah?"

The waiter replied, "She's home cooking." (She's at home and she's cooking.)

1003. Mailman: "I've got a letter here, but the name on the envelope is OBLITERATED."

Man with small vocabulary: "It can't be me. My name is SMITH.

1004. Two drunks were walking along a railroad rack.

One drunk said, "These steps are pretty steep, aren't they?

The other drunk said, ""That's nothing. It's the low handrail that bothers me."

1005. Two patients and a nurse were sitting on a bench in the front yard of a mental institution. A rather large bird flew over and let go with a somewhat messy deposit which landed on one of the patient's bald head.

The nurse, worried for fear this would throw the patient into a fit, explained loudly, "Now, Charlie, you just stay right where you are and don't get upset. I'm going to run and get some toilet paper. I'll be right back."

Charlie sat perfectly still. Finally he slowly turned his head to the other patient. Rolling his eyes in the direction of he departed nurse, he said, "I do believe that nurse has gone crazy. That bird will be 50 miles away from here by the time she gets back with that toilet paper."

1006. Q. Did you hear about the formal dance at the zoo?

A. The penguins came in tuxedos and the monkeys came in tails.

1007. A young girl was getting tired of going steady with her boyfriend. While they were sitting together, he said, "There isn't anyone else, is there?"

She replied, "Oh, there must be !"

1008. Q. What rock group gets clothes the whitest?

A. The Bleach Boys

1009. Q. Why did he moron eat a light bulb?

A. Because he wanted a light snack.

1010. Q. What is a hamburger's motto?

A. If at first you don't succeed, FRY, FRY, AGAIN.

1011. Do something. Lead, follow, or get out of the way.

1012. Q. Why did the boy wear only one boot?

A. Because he head that the snow outside would only be one foot deep.

1013. Employee: "I'd like a leave of absence to get married."

Boss: "You just came back from vacation. Why didn't you get married during your vacation?

Employee: ""What! And ruin my vacation!"

1014. Q. When do cows reire?

A. When they have utter disability. (udder)

1015.   "Give him enough rope, and he'll hang a joke on it."

   --W. C. Fields –

1016.   A family (in the 1920s) lived next door to a Mom and POP grocery store. The family was not used to planning ahead; whenever they needed an item, they'd just run next door and get it.

   One day the father was sitting on the toilet and he noticed there was no toilet paper either on the roll or in the cupboard beneath the sink. He yelled downstairs to his daughter, "Jane, will you run next door and get me a roll of toilet paper?"

   "Okay, Daddy," she replied.

   Little Jane went next door and saw a long line of people patiently waiting in line. She promptly walked to the head of the line and asked in a loud voice, "Mrs. Morfy, Could I please have a roll of toilet paper?"

   Mrs. Morfy said, "Jane, you'll have to wait your turn."

   Little Jane replied in a loud voice, "But my daddy is waiting for it."

1017.   Two men were at a convention in a large city, and they had a few hours to themselves. Their names were John and Joe.

   John said to Joe: "How about playing gin rummy?"

   Joe said, "I tried it once and didn't like it."

   John said, "How about playing pool?"

   Joe said, "I tried it once and didn't like it."

   John said, "Well, how about going to a movie?"

   Joe said, "No, I tried that once and didn't like it. Besides, my son is coming to visit me this afternoon."

   John said, "Your only child, I pesume!"

1018. Two men named Rigor and Mortis worked in a morgue in a large city. A new body was just brought in on a gurney. Rigor began examining the contents of the dead man's pockets. Shortly, he exclaimed, "Oh man! Look Mortis! This guy has the winning lottery ticket in his pocket!"

Mortis looked at the ticket, rolled his eyes and yelled, "Lucky stiff!"

1019. May the worst of times in your future be the same as the best times in your past. (Scotch blessing)

1020. It took a long time for the husband to get his domineering wife to see a psychiatrist.

After she came back home, the husband asked, "Did you make any progress?"

"Not much," she said. "It took me 50 minutes to convince him that the couch would look better up against the wall."

1021. A man was scheduled to have a heart transplant operation. His heart doctor said to him, "I'm going to give you a choice of two hearts. You can have the heart of a 20 year athlete or the heart of a 50 year old IRS man."

The man said, "I'll choose he latter –he heart of the 50 year old IRS man."

The doctor asked, "Why?"

The man said, "I want a heart that has not been used."

1022. A little boy had just returned home from a funeral. He asked, "Mommy, is it true that we come from dust and go back to dust?"

"Yes," his mother said.

"You'd better look under my bed," he said. "Someone is either coming or going."

1023. Doctor, "Did you follow my diections by drinking waer 15 minutes before going to bed?"

Patient: "I tried to, but I was full after five minutes."

1024. A henpecked husband had an automobile accident. The police officer asked him "How did this accident happen?"

The henpecked husband explained, "You see, my wife fell asleep in the back seat."

1025. Q. What is something that loses its head in the daytime, but gets it back at night?

A. A pillow

1026. A boy was doing poorly in math in a public high school; his grades were Ds and Fs. So his parents decided to send him to a private Christian school. They lived within easy walking distance from the school.

While there the boy studied math every day, both during school hours and at home in the evenings. At the end of the semester he had As in math—for both the semester grade and final exam.

His father asked, "What motivated you to do so well in math?"

He replied, "When I saw that mostly naked guy nailed to a plus sign, I knew they meant business"

1027. Customer: "I need some apples for my husband. Have these apples been sprayed with poison?"

Grocery clerk: "No, you'll have to get that at the drug store."

1028. 1st henpecked man: "Who's in charge at your house?"

2nd henpecked man: Well, my wife takes care of the bird, the cat, and the dog. But I can say what I want to he goldfish."

1029. 1st girl: "I caught my boyfriend flirting."

2nd girl: "I caught my boyfriend that way too."

1030. Q. What is the difference between an outlaw and a church bell?

A. One steals from the people, and the other peals for the people.

1031. Q. What did the witch say to the twin witches?

A. Which witch is which?

1032. Q. What do you call a witch on the beach?

A. A sand witch. (a sandwich)

1033. Q. On which street do witches live?

A. On a dead end street.

1034. Q. Why was Samson the greatest actor in the Bible?

A. He brought the house down.

1035. Drop a stone into the water.

In a moment it is gone,

But there are a hundred ripples

Going on and on.

Say an unkind word.

In a moment it is gone.

But there are a hundred ripples

Going on and on.

Say a few words of praise or cheer.

IIn a moment it is gone.

But there are a hundred ripples

Going on and on.-- Anonymous –

1036. Q. Why is that hill the dead center of this county?

A. Because it is a cemetery.

1037. Q. Why did the Amish woman divorce her husband?

A. He was driving her buggy.

1038. On a beautiful blue and gold October day, two green leaves were hanging on a branch. They were the only two leaves left on this branch. One leaf said to the other, "You know, I've worked hard all my life changing carbon dioxide and water into glucose and oxygen. Now I'm looking forward to retirement. In fact, my wife and I have always wanted to do some traveling."

The other leaf said, "Oh yeah! Where to?"

"Oh, possibly down to the ground."

1039. A man wobbled up to the ticket counter at the airport. He said to the clerk, "How long of a hang over will I have in Chicago?" (lay over)

1040. Q. What are three short words associated with being sick? A. ILL, PILL, BILL

1041. Q. Why did the farmer cross a cow with an octopus?

A. To get a do-it-yourself milker,

1042. Joe: "Did you hear about the sale on camouflage paint?

Mole: "No. How did it go?"

Joe: "Not so well. They could not find the paint."

1043. Jeff: "Here's one final question of my survey, Biff. What is your opinion concerning student apathy here at the high school?"

Biff: "Who cares?"

1044. Q. Why do spiders get dizzy?

A. They are always spinning.

1045. Teacher (calling on student not paying attention):

" Johnny, define ignorance and apathy."

Johnny: "I don't know and I don't care."

Teacher: (flustered and blushing) "Inadvertently, you have given two good examples," she finally said.

1046. 1st auto mechanic: "Which do you prefer for upholstery in a car –leather or fabric?"

2nd auto mechanic: "Fabric. Leather is too hard to wipe your hands on." (Don't hire this guy.)

1047. Marriage is like a cafeteria. You pick out something that looks good, and you pay for it down the line.

1048. "Joe: Did you hear about the kidnapping?"

Moe: "No."

Joe: "He woke up." (kid napping)

1049. A man was making a telephone call at a pay telephone. The operator said, "That will be $12.88 please."

The man replied, "I told you to reverse he charges."

The operator then said, "O.K., that will be $88.12."

1050. Q. What is the daffynition of garden hose?

A. Socks worn in the garden.

1051. Q. Why should you feed garlic to your baby?

A. So your baby will be easier to find in the dark.

1052. A young man went into the lingerie department to buy a brassiere for his new wife. He was very embarrassed. He found a clerk and tried to explain what he wanted.

Clerk: "What size?"

Young man: "I don't know."

Clerk: "The size of a grapefruit?"

Young man: "No. Smaller."

Clerk: "The size of oranges or apples?"

Young man: "No. Smaller."

Clerk: "The size of eggs?"

Young man: "Yeah! Yeah! Fried!"

1053. Q. How did the moron break his legs raking leaves?

A. He fell out of the tree.

1054. A man had gone fishing, but he did not catch anything. On the way home he stopped at the fish market.

He said to the clerk, "Throw me six of the biggest fish you have."

The clerk asked, "Why should I throw them to you?"

The man said, "I want to catch them. I'm a lousy fisherman, but I am not a liar."

1055. /Q. What is the best way to make a fire with two sticks?

A. Make sure one of them is a match.

1056. Q. How many paranoids does it take to change a light bulb?

A. Who wants to know?

1057. In a large crowd an old man passed out and dropped to the ground. Someone seeing him yelled, "Does anyone know VCR?" (CPR – cardiac pulmonary resuscitation)

1058. An old lady walked up to an old man in a nursing home and said, "If you drop your pants, I can tell your age."

So the old man dropped his pants, and she said, "You're eighty-three."

The old man said, "You're right! How could you tell?"

The old lady said, "You told me yesterday."

1059. A Russian man went to a car deal in Moscow and ordered a car. He asked the salesman, "How long will it take for me to get the car?"

The salesman said, "Ten years." Then he showed the date on a calendar.

The Russian man asked, "Morning or afternoon?"

The salesman became angry. He yelled, "What difference does it make? Morning or afternoon!"

The Russian man explained, "But the plumber is coming in the morning."

1060. Patient: "I see weird creatures coming out from underneath my bed. What can I do about it?"

Doctor: "Saw the legs off your bed."

1061. Q. What do you call a female horse that is awake in the dark?
A. A nightmare (night mare)

1062. Q. Where does an Eskimo keep his money?

A/ In a snowbank.

ACRONYMS – Not an everyday word. I had to consult a dictionary: "A letter formed from the initial letter or letters or each of the successive parts or major parts of a compound term."

YUPPIES ----------- Young, urban professional

BUPPIES ------------ Black, urban professional

HUPPIES ------------ Hispanic, urban professional

GUPPIES ------------ Gay, urban professional

PUPPIES ------------ Pregnant, urban professional

SUPPIES ------------ Senior, urban professional

OPALS --------------- Older people with active lifestyles

GRUMP - Grim, ruthless, upwardly mobile professional

DINK ---------------- Double income, no kids

SITCOM - Single income, two kids, outrageous mortgage

MINKS --------------- Multiple income, no kids

DINKS --------------- Dual income with kids

TICKS --------------- Two income couple, kids

OINKS --------------- One income, no kids

1063. Joe: "Why are you walking around with two pairs of glasses on?"

Moe: "I'm trying to find the 6th dimension."

1064. Jack: "I heard your uncle went on a safari in Africa and did not return."

Mack: "Yes. Something he disagreed with ate him."

1065. Q. What did the beaver say to the t ree?

A. It's been nice gnawing you. (knowing)

1066. A tourist climbed over a fence and saw a bull. He yelled to a farmer on the other side of the fence, "Is the bull safe?"

The farmer yelled back, "A darn sight safer than you are."

1067. Patient: "Before I came here I saw a fortuneteller, a palm reader, and an astrologer."

Doctor: "And what foolish advice did they give you?"

Patient: "They all told me to come and see you."

1068. Joe: "Mrs. Bigger had a baby. Who was bigger—Mrs. Bigger or her baby?

Moe: "Mrs. Bigger."

Joe: "No. That's wrong. It's her baby."

Moe: "Why?"

Moe:"Because he was a little Bigger." (Is your head spinning?)

1069. Q. What is the daffynition of the word MUMMY?

A. An Egyptian pressed for time.

1070. Q. What did the rug say to the floor?

A. Don't worry. I've got you covered.

Q. What did the wall say to the adjacent wall?

A. I'll meet you at the corner.

1071. The following inscription was found on an 18th century dinner plate:

"Earth I am.

It is most true.

Disdain me not

For so are you." (anonymous)

1072. Two old ladies were sitting side by side in a church. One old lady looked at the other and whispered, "You've got a suppository in your ear."

The other old lady said, "What did you say?"

The first old lady raised her voice, "You've got a suppository in your ear." People in the immediate vicinity began turning around and staring at these two old ladies.

The deaf lady said, "I still can't hear you. Shout it!"

The first old lady yelled, "You've got a suppository in you ear." At this outburst everyone in the church turned around and stared.

Then the deaf lady said in a loud voice, "Now I know where I put my hearing aid!

1073. Oliver Hardy: "You know, Stan, she [Olive's new wife] thinks I think more of you than I do of her."

      Stan Laurel: "Well you do, don't you?"

      Stan: "I'm a nip and tuck drinker."

      Oliver: "How so?"

      Stan: "One nip and you can tuck me in for the night."

1074. Q. What is the daffynition of geneology?

      A. Tracing yourself back to people better than you.

1075. A man and a woman had just met at a dance. She casually asked about his plans for the rest of the evening.

      He said, "I'm going to find myself a hot tomato. I'm going to ask her to my apartment, mix her a few drinks, put her on the couch, turn out the lights, and make mad passionate love to he. What do you think of that idea?"

      The woman smiled and said, "It sounds like a great idea, if you ask me."

1076. A young man who claimed to be a surfing enthusiast went down to the beach one day. He waded out into the water a few feet and stood there. His new friend said to him, "Come on. Show me how you can surf."

      The young man said, "I don't have to."

      "Why not?"

      The young man said, "They only <u>surf</u> who only stand and wait." (serve –John Milton)

1077. Q. What kind of a hen lays the longest?

      A. A dead hen.

1078. Jack: "I'm a self-made man."

      Mack: "That means you have to take all the blame."

1079. A man named Amos always weighed his decisions very carefully. He would always make a though discussion of any topic. He would commence speaking by saying "On the one hand" and continue for a long time; then he would say "On the other hand and continue for an equally long time. As a result, he did nothing.

On his tombstone, beneath his name and dates, they carved a big ZERO – 0.

1080. A brash and aggressive young man went into a bank and said, "I want to see the president of this bank."

The secretary asked, "Do you have an appointment?"

"No," he said as he rushed past her and right into the president's office.

He said to he president of the bank, "Are you people running out of money?"

"Why no," the president said, "We have assets of over four hundred million dollas."

The young man exclaimed, "In a pig's eye, you haven't!"

The president retorted, "And what makes you think we haven't?"

The young man replied, "Because every check I've written has come back marked INSUFFICIENT FUNDS."

1081. Q. Why are the Egyptian pyramids he best place to look for a mother?

A. Because that's where the rich mummies live.

1082. Q. What is the richest car in the world?

A. An Old sMobile (Oldsmobile)

1083.   Two teenage girls were talking on the telephone with each other on the last day of summer vacation. Their names were Jean and Jill.

Jean: "What a rotten summer, Jill! I didn't do anything special. I didn't meet any guys! I didn't even get a tan!"

Jill: "Same with me. This is one summer I'd like to forget!"

Jean: "So would I?"

Jill: "But why does it have to end?"

1084.   Some people are good losers. Others can't act.

1085.   School guidance counselor: "Did you always hate going to school?"

Student: "No."

Counselor: "When did you like going o school?"

Student: "The first day of first grade. That was before they told me I had o come back the next day."

1086.   If the climbing is getting easy, you're not climbing.

1087.   Two men and a moron wanted to get into the Olympics.

Q. The first man carried a long pipe. In what sport was he interested?

A. Pole vaulting.

Q. The second man was carrying a man-hole cover. In what sport was he interested?

A. Throwing the discus.

Q. The moron was carrying a roll of barbed wire. What was his sport?

A. Fencing.

1088.   Never let yesterday use up today.

1089.   However you live, it will show in your face.

1090.   The treasurer of the Ladies' Aid Society in the small town took some of their money to the bank to deposit it. "Here's the <u>Aid</u> money," the lady said to the teller."

The teller thought she said <u>Egg</u> money and replied,"I see the old hens did pretty well this week."

1091.   President Coolidge was a man of few words and aptly named "Silent Cal." Here's a little story which proves the point.

One Sunday morning after President Coolidge had returned to the White House from church, where he had gone alone. Mrs. Coolidge inquired, "Was the sermon good?"

"Yes."

"What was it about?" she asked.

"Sin."

"What did he minister say about it?"

"He was against it."

1092.   We can only be youngonce, but with humor we can be immature forever.

1093.   Mr. and Mrs. Lockhorn returned early from a vacation. As they were unloading the trunk of their car, a neighbor lady came over and inquired, "I thought you were coming back next Monday. What happened?"

Mrs. Lockhorn replied, "We came back early, because we had about as much fun as we could stand."

1094.   Q. How come morons don't become pharmacists?

A. Because they can't fit the little bottle [vial] in the typewriter.

1095.   A disgruntled college student went to his professor's office to complain about his grade.

Student: "Professor, I've got to protest. I don't think I deserve this zero on my test."

Professor: "I agree with you."

Student: His jaw dropped. "Then why did you write a zero on my test?"

Professor: "A zero is the lowest grade I am permitted to give."

1096. Old man: "I used to make men's underwear. But now I'm broke."

Young man: "What happened?"

Old man: "The bottom fell out."

1097. Q. What do you call a cow lying on the ground?

A. Ground beef.

1098. Q. Why did the football player ask the coach to flood the field?

A. So he could go in as a sub.

1099. "Yes, ma'am," the old one-legged salt confided to the inquisitive lady. I fell over the side of the ship, and a shark came along and grabbed me by the leg."

"Mercy!" the lady gasped. "And what did you do?"

"I let him have the leg, of course, ma'am. I never argue with sharks."

1100. Patient: "It's really disturbing. I can't remember the street I live on."

Psychiatrist: "Don't worry. It's probably a mental block."

1101. Biology teacher: "Define the term SPINE."

Class clown: "Your spine is a long limber bone. You head sits on one end of it, and you sit on the other"

Biology teacher: "Define BACTERIA."

Class clown:"Back door of a cafeteria."

1102. Doctor: "After surgery, you can pay me $500 down and then $300 a month."

Patient: "That's like buying a car."

Doctor: "That's right. I am."

1103. A student who continually looked at the clock during class, began to get on the teacher's nerves. The next time the class met, there was a sign over the clock that read: TIME WILL PASS. WILL YOU?

1104. A passerby noticed a hand-printed sign in a store window that said: HARD WEAR She went into the store and informed the proprietor of the misspelling. After he thanked her, she wandered around the store and made a few purchases.

After she paid for her purchase, she asked, "Aren't you going to correct the spelling on your sign?"

"Goodness, no!" exclaimed the store owner. "Everyone who comes in here to correct my spelling, buys something."

1105. The successful inventor loved to invite guests to his home to demonstrate his labor-saving devices. After the tour, guests had to pass through a heavy turnstile that proved to be a test of physical strength for most of them. One asked, "Why, with all these modern devices, do you still maintain such a heavy turnstile

"It's a simple invention," explained he inventor. "Everyone who pushes through the turnstile pumps ten gallons of water into my roof tank."

1106. A hungry tramp walked up to an imposing house and rang the bell. A haughty lady opened the door just a few inches. "What is it?" she demanded in a loud voice.

"Lady, could you give me a job so I could earn some money to buy a hot meal? I haven't eaten all day."

The lady replied, "It just so happens that I have two gallons of green paint. If you paint the <u>porch</u> out back, I'll see that you have all he dinner you can eat."

Two hours later, the man reappeared at the front door. He said, "Well, I finished the job. But that's no <u>Porsche</u>, lady, it's a Ferrari!

1107. The new Army bride was showing her gifts to a friend. "I just love personalized gifts like these towels marked HIS and HERS. And here's my very favorite—an olive-drab blanket with U S printed right in the center."

1108. Two old ladies occupied adjacent beds in a room in the nursing home. An old man in a wheelchair was visiting them. Suddenly the two women began arguing about the window. Hearing their loud voices, a nurse's aide stepped into the room.

"If this window is opened, one lady declared, "I shall catch cold and probably die"

"If the window is shut," the other lady announced, "I shall certainly suffocate." The two old ladies glared at each other.

The nurse's aide didn't know what to do. She shrugged her shoulders.

The old man in the wheelchair said to the nurse's aide, "First, open the window. That will kill one of them. Next, shut it. That will kill the other. Then we can have some peace."

1109. Teacher: "Where is your homework?"

Smart aleck student "I don't have it, teach. My dog ate it."

Teacher: "Just how could your dog eat your homework?"

Smart aleck stdent: "I fed it to him."

1110.   Dear Abby: Having just read your column about how some people murder the English language, here are some examples taken from actual letters received by the local welfare department in applications for support.

   1.   "I am forwarding my marriage certificate and six children. I had seven, but one died which was baptized on a half sheet of paper."

   2.   "Mrs. Jones has not had any clothes for a year and a half, and has been visited regularly by the clergy."

   3.   "I am glad to report that husband who is missing is dead."

   4.   "I am very annoyed to find that you brand my son illiterate. This is a dirty lie, as I was married a week before he was born."

   5.   "Please find out for certain if my husband is dead. The man I am living with can' eat or do anything until he knows."

   6.   "I am forwarding my marriage certificate and three children, one of which is a mistake as you can see."

   7.   "My husband got his project cut off two weeks ago, and I haven't had any relief since."

   8.   "Unless I get my husband's pretty soon, I will be forced to live an immortal life."

9. "You have changed my little boy to a girl. Will this make a difference?"

10. "I have no children as yet as my husband is a truck driver and works day and night."

11. "I want money quick as I can get it. I have been in bed with the doctor for two weeks, and he doesn't do me any good."(Lillian Armet, Far Rockaway, New York)

1111. Joe: "We were so poor I didn't have pants to wear."Moe: "Not even jeans?"

Joe: "Hers wouldn't fit me either."

1112. Patient: "I'm a light eater, Doctor."

Doctor: "You weigh over three hundred pounds. How can you be a light eater?"

Patient: ""Easy. As soon as it gets light I start eating."

1113. Patient: "I got rid of 198 pounds of ugly fat."

Doctor: "How did you do that?"

Patient: "I divorced my husband."

1114. Patient: "Every time I drink coffee I get a stabbing pain in my right eye. How come?"

Doctor: "Take the spoon out of your cup."

1115. Joe: "I've been seeing spots before my eyes."

1116. Moe: "Did you see a doctor?"

Joe: "No. Just spots."

1117. Q. Why didn't Abe Lincoln receive his mail in Washington?"

A. Don't you remember his Gettysburg Address?

1118. A man in prison was telling his cell mate the story of his life. He said, "Well, my first wife died from eating poisoned mushrooms. And my second wife died from eating poisoned mushrooms. And my third wife died…"

His cell mate interrupted. "And did your third wife die from a similar cause?"

"No. Her death was due to a concussion. She would not eat the poisoned mushrooms."

1119. Joe: "I fell off a fifty foot ladder."

Moe: "How come you didn't get hurt?

Joe: "I fell off the first rung."

Moe: "I'd say you are climbing pretty high for humor."

1120. A wealthy eccentric old farmer in Texas had a large pool constructed on his property. He erected a sign: DANGER. NO SWIMMING ALLOWED.

One hot muggy day, while standing on his deck, he heard laughter and splashing from the direction of the pool.

He hobbled out to the pool and saw a bunch of young women and young men skinny dipping. When they saw the farmer, they all swam to the deep end. One of them shouted to him, "We're not coming out until you leave."

The old man replied, "I didn't come out her to watch you swim or make you get out of the pool naked."

One of the men yelled, "Then, why did you come?" Go away and let us have fun."

The old man said, "I'm here to feed the alligator."

1121. Patient: "Every time I put on this hat, I hear music."

Doctor: "Give me your hat." Then the doctor turned the hat over and took out the band.. (an ugly pun!)

1122. Tom: "Do you have any money in the bank?"

 Dick: "I don't know."

 Tom: "Well, why don't you know?"

 Dick: "Because I haven't shaken it lately."

1123. Q. What did the frog say after eating his meal?

 A. Time sure is fun when you're having flies.

1124. Q. What are you supposed to do if you see an endangered animal eating an endangered plant?

 A. That's like watching your worst enemy drive over the cliff in your new Cadillac.

1125. Q. Why was 6 sad?

 A. Because 7 <u>8</u> 9 (ate

1126. Q. What did the beaver say to the tree?

 A. Good bye. It's been nice gnawing you. (knowing)

1127. Q. If you have 365 used condoms, what can you do with them?

 A. Put them in a tire and call it a Good Year.

1128. Joe: "My hen lays eggs."

 Moe: "What's so great about that?"

 Joe: "Can you do it?"

1129. She's a lady carpenter. You should see her build.

 She's a lady lawyer. You should see her biefs.

1130. A silly young man from the Clyde

 In a funeral carriage was spied.

 When asked who was dead

 He giggled and said,

 "I don't know. I just came for the ride."

1131.   Q. If a geologist finds a new mineral under lime, what does he call it?

A. Sublime.

1132.   Q. Why do old geologists never die?

A. They just petrify.

1133.   Q. How do you test the strength of an electromagnet?

A. Have it pump iron.

1134.   A dashing young salesman visited a church youth meeting and fell in love with a deacon's daughter. After a few dates, he decided to get a character report before proposing marriage. So he hired a detective.

After a week of probing, the detective gave his report:

Fine reputation, No past scandals, Gentle, Even –tempered, Excellent health, Many church-going friends. The only mark on her character is that recently she's been seen with a salesman of doubtful reputation.

1135.   Q. Why does that man have holes in his socks?

A. Because he's married to a woman who doesn't give a darn.

1136.   Q. What three animals are always found in political debates?.

A. A donkey, an elephant, and a lot of bull.

Q. What are a woman's three favorite animals?

A. A mink on her back, a Jaguar in the garage, and a tiger in bed.

1137.   Q. A father worked hard all his life to keep the wolf away from the door. Why was he angry with his daughter when she began dating?

A. She brought one home.

1138. Q. Why should prayers never be taken out of the public schools?

A. That's how a lot of the students get through.

1139. A bather whose clothing was strewed

By winds that left her quite nude

Saw a man coming along.

And unless I am wrong,

You expected this line to be lewd.

1140. SIGNS

ON a school bulletin board: Free! Knowledge on Mondays through Fridays. Bring your own container.

In a bakery shop window: Oh What Foods

These morsels be.

1141. Q. What is the definition of credit.

A. A clever financial trick that enables us to

Spend what we haven't got.

1142. After the bank was robbed for the third time, an FBI man came to make an investigation. He asked a teller, Did you notice anything unusual about the robber?"

The teller replied, "Yes, he seemed to be better dressed each time."

1143. Q. What is the daffynition of a genius?

A. A crackpot who makes a screwball idea work.

1144. Customer (at perfume counter).: "Be honest. Does this stuff really work?

Saleslady: "If this stuff really worked, would I be standing here eight hours a day?"

1145. Sign on a church bulletin board: THE LORD LOVES A CHEERFUL GIVER. HE ALSO ACCEPTS MONEY FROM A GROUCH.

1146. Sign in a loan office. WE WILL LOAN YOU ENOUGH MONRY TO GET YOU COMPLETELY OUT OF DEBT.

1147. Q. What did the beaver say to the tree?

A. So long. It's been nice gnawing you.

1148. Q. What is the daffynition of a platonic relationship?

A. Mind over mattress.

Q. What is the daffynition of diet?

A. Mind over platter.

1149. A one-armed man walked into a barber shop. The barber said to him, "Haven't I shaved you before?

The man replied, "No. I got my arm cut off in a saw mill accident."

1150. Q. What did on math book say to the other math book?

A. Don't bother me. I've got my own problems.

1151. Q. Why is the dog such a lovable creature?

A. Because he wags his tail instead of his tongue.

1152. Q. How do you communicate with a fish?

A. Drop him a line. (Hear the groans.)

1153. Q. When does a ghost sleep?

A. When he is dead tired.

1154. Q. What is it like to be kissed by a vampire?

A. It's a pain in the neck.

1155. Prisoner: "But, Judge, I wasn't drunk. I was just drinking."

Judge: "Okay. I won't give you a month in jail. I'll give you just thirty days."

1156. Teacher: "Tom, I want you to use the word archaic in a sentence."

Tom: "I wish I could have our cake and eat it too."

1157. She's so modest that she blushes when she hears the word intersection.

1158. On a cold October night two drunk hoboes were sleeping outside in a farmer's field. They got so cold that one of them got up and closed the farmer's gate.

1159. "Few sinners are saved after the first twenty minutes of the sermon." (Mark Twain)

1160. Q. Why did the moron plant Cheerios in his yard?

A. Because he wanted to grow donuts?

1161. Two drunks went into a zoo and stopped in front of a lion's cage. The lion opened his mouth wide and roared.

One drunk said, "We'd better get out of here."

The other drunk said, "No. I'm staying for the movie."

1162. A young man was rescued from the top floor of an eight story building by jumping into a big net that the firemen held for him.

Afterwards, someone asked him, "Did all he sins of your life flash before your eyles?"

He answered honestly. "No. I only fell eight stories—not enough time."

1163. Two men went into a diner. They sat down on stools and ordered two glasses of milk. One man said to the waitress, "Make sure mine is in a clean glass." Then he laughed, mocking the busy woman.

The woman brought the two classes of milk and set them down on the counter. Then she said, "Now, which one of you wanted the clean glass?"

1164.   Two mice died and went to heaven. They asked St. Peter, "What do you have to eat?"

St. Peter said, "Put on these roller skates and look around."

The mice put on their roller skates and took off.

Then, two cats died and went to heaven. They asked St Pete, "What do you have to eat?"

"For you," St. Peter said, "We have meals on wheels."

1165.   Q. Do you know why a man can't starve on the desert?

A. Because of the sand which is there. (sandwich)

1166.   A man had attended a dinner where there were many women wearing very low cut evening dresses. His wife did not go to this dinner. When he got home, his wife asked casually, "What were the women wearing?"

He blushed and said, "I don't know. I didn't look under the table."

1167.   Q. Why is a doctor like a stork?

A. They both have big bills.

1168.   Q. Why are soldiers tired on April Fool's Day?

A. They've just had a thirty-one day March.

1169.   Q. Why did he soldier salute the TV set?

A Because it was General Electric.

1170.   Imitation is the sincerest kind of flattery.

1171.   Pan handler (begging): "Can I have $10,000 for a for a cup of coffee?"

Rich man: "Why do you need that much money?

Pan handler: "You see, I like to go to a drive-in, and I don't have no car."

1172. Q. What runs 2000 miles and has 4 eyes? (I's)

A The Mississippi River.

1173. A mommy sardine and her baby sardine were swimming, and a sardine came by. The baby asked, "What is that, Mommy?"

Mommy replied, "That's a submarine You should see how they pack people in there."

1174. A little girl and a little boy were strolling along a beach. They stopped, took off their clothes, and continued walking along the beach.

The little boy looked down at the little girl and said, "I didn't know there was that much difference between Catholics and Protestants."

1175. Joe: "Did you meet yur uncle at the station?"

Moe: "No. I've known him all my life."

1176. It's amazing how many people are shocked by honesty and so few by deceit.

1177. Jane: "How do you get your late night visitors to go home?"
Sally: "I walk through the room, holding a box of breakfast cereal."

1178. Home–Ec teacher: "When the sauce begins to simmer, I add a tablespoon full of water."

Miss Smarty: "Level or heaping?"

1179. An actor was playing a death scene. His director interrupted him by yelling, "Put some life into it. You're supposed to be dying."

1180. History teacher: "When was the Iron Age?"

Class clown: "That was before wash and wear."

1181.   Q. Why did the Indians settle America first?

A. They had reservations.

1182.   New employer to be: "I hope you are not a clock watcher."

New employee to be: "Certainly not. I don't like inside work. I'm a whistle listener."

1183.   Q. What did one SCUBA diver say to another SCUBA diver?

A. "Where's the reef? [Wendy's ad—Where's the beef?]

1184.   Q. How do you know that clocks are shy?

A. Their hands are always in front of their face.

1185.   Q. What did the priest say when the cow walked into the church?

A. Holy COW!

1186.   Q. How do football players cool off?

A. They stand in front of their fans.

1187.   Q. What do you call a scared SCUBA diver?

A. Chicken of the Sea

1188.   Doctor: "You are too wide around your middle. I'm putting you on a diet of lettuce, carrots, celery, and green onions."

Patient: ""Do I eat that before or after meals?"

1189.   The obnoxious lady customer in the department store said to the clerk waiting on her, "Isn't there a smarter clerk who can wait on me?"

The clerk replied, "No, Madam. "All the smart clerks ducked out when they saw you coming."

1190.   Q. Why aren't elephants allowed on the beach?

A. Because they can't keep their trunks up.

1191.   Tom: "There's one good thing about smog."

Dick: "What's that?"

Tom: "At least, you can see what you are breathing."

1192. George: "Gracie, what's this check stub—one pullover, $25.00. I don't mean to sound like a cheapskate, but isn't that a lot of money for a pullover?"

Gracie: "The man on the motorcycle said it was the regular price."

George: "You got it from a man on a motorcycle?"

Gracie: "Yes, I went through a red light and he dove up and said, "Pull over" {Radio: George Burns and Gracie Allen)

1193. Joe: "I'm never going to gamble again."

Moe: "I don't believe it."

Joe: "How much do you want to bet?"

Moe: "You blew it."

1194. The one time you don't want to fail is the last time you try. (Charles Kettering)

1195. A young man went to the court house information desk and said, "I want a license."

The clerk asked him, "Do you want a hunting license?"

He replied, "No. A marriage license. I've been hunting long enough."

1196. It was the first day of school, and a new student, Toshiba, the son of a Japanese businessman, entered the fourth grade. The teacher greeted the class and said, "Let's begin by reviewing some American history. Who said, 'Give me liberty or give me death?"

She saw only a sea of blank faces except for that of Toshiba, who had his hand up. "Patrick Henry, 1775" said the boy.

"Now," said the teacher, "Who said 'government of the people, by the people, and for the people shall not perish from the earth'"?

Again, no response except from Toshiba: "Abraham Lincoln, 1863."

The teacher snapped at the class. "You should be ashamed. Toshiba, who is new to our country, knows more about it than you do."

As she turned to write something on the blackboard, she heard a loud whisper, "Damned Japanese!"

"Who said that?" she demanded.

Toshiba put his hand up. "Lee Iacocca, 1982," he said.

(Dick Campbell—Reader's Digest, October, 1991)

1197. The answer is: "Chicken Teriyake." Now, what is the question?"

The question is: Name the only surviving Kamikaze pilot.

(Robert Ireland, Dearborn, Michigan)

1198. Q. Why aren't there any vampires who are vegetarians?

A. Because they can't get blood out of a turnip.

1199. Q. What does a vampire order in a bar?

A. A blood light

1200. Student: "I'd like to publicly apologize for my behavior during physics class".

Teacher: "Thank you. I accept your apology."

Student: "It was childish, immature, selfish, and disruptive. I meant to save it for math class."

1201. Q. Why do surgeons wear masks when they do surgery?

A. Because if they make a mistake no one will know who did it.

1202. Q. Did you hear the joke about quicksand?

A. I did but it takes a long time to sink in.

1203. Q. Why is the letter T like an island?

A. Because it is in the middle of water. (waTer)

1204. A pharmacist handed a vial of pills to his elderly white-haired customer. He said, "Take one of these pills every four hours or as often as you can get the cap off."

1205. Teacher: "Jimmy, weren't you absent yesterday?"

Jimmy: "Yes, ma'am."

Teacher: "Well, you're supposed to bring a note from home whenever you miss school."

Jimmy: "I know."

Teacher: "Well, then, why didn't you bring the note?"

Jimmy: "But I didn't miss school at all."

1206. Sign on a student's T-shirt: I LOVE SCHOOLWHEN IT IS CLOSED

1207. Q. What is a gourmet?

A. A man who, when invited out for an evening of wine, women, and song, asks "What kind of wine?"

1208. Diner (finding a wasp in his soup) asks the waiter, "What's that?"

Waiter: "Vitamin Bee."

1209. A politician made his usual speech. During the question and answer session afterwards, a young man raised his hand and asked a question.

The politician said, "I wish I had an answer to that question, because I am tired of answering that question."

1210. Q. Where are some of the best bedtime stories found? A. In motel registers—Mr. & Mrs. Smith, Mr.& Mrs. Jones, Etc. (Bob Ireland, Dearborn, Michigan)

1211. Q. What did the beaver say to the tree?

A. So long. It's been nice gnawing you. (seeing you)

1212. Q. What did the nurse say to the invisible man?

A. The doctor can't see you now.

1213. Q. What is the difference between a drunk man and a dead man?

A. A drunk man carries his beer. In the case of the dead man, the bier carries him. (beer, bier)

1214. Q. What do you call a cow that does not give milk?

A. An udder failure. (udder, utter)

1215. Q. What is a hug?

A. A round-about way of showing affection

1216. Q. Why did the Amish woman divorce her husband? A. He was driving her buggy.

1217. Q. What is the chief product of the Amish farms?

A. Children

1218. Lady: "Can you give me a room and a bath?

Hotel clerk: "I'll give you a room, but you'll have to take your own bath."

1219. Wife: "What was the name of the hotel we stayed in--in Duluth?

Husband: "I can't remember right now. But, wait while I look through my towels."

1220. A man was being examined by a doctor. One of the doctor's questions was, "Do you have intercourse?"

The man scratched his head and then said, "Wait a minute." He walked to the door leading to the waiting room, opened it, and yelled out to his wife, "Hey, Gladys, do we have intercourse?"

Gladys replied, "No. We've got Blue Cross and Blue Shield."

1221. Q. What is a shark's favorite sandwich?

A. A peanut butter and jellyfish sandwich.

1222. Joe: "My eyes are running, my nose is dripping like a faucet, my throat's clogging up. Maybe I should see a doctor?"

Moe: "Sounds more like you should see a plumber."

1223. Diner (to waitress): "I'd like a piece of that pecan pie."

Waitress: "Shoo fly, shoo fly. Sir, that ain't no pecan pie. That's apple pie."

1224. Q. Is it hard to milk a cow?

A. No, any jerk can do it.

1225. Customer: "I'd like to buy some apples."

Clerk: "How about some Baldwins?"

Customer: "Okay. I never did like hairy apples."

1226. Q. What's worse than raining cats and dogs?

A. Hailing taxi cabs.

1227. Q. How many waffles can you eat?

A. A waffle lot.

1228. Q. Why did the moron want to sleep in the fireplace?

A.. Because he wanted to sleep like a log?

1229. Q. Why was Cinderella thrown off the baseball

team?

A. Because she ran away from the ball.

1230. Q. What did one tonsil say to the other tonsil?

A. Get ready. The doctor is taking us out tonight.

1231. Knock knock.

Who's there?

Roach.

Roach who?

Wrote you a letter but you did not answer.

1232. A man received a prescription from his doctor. On the way to the drug store, he asked his friend to see if he could read it.

His friend looked at the illegible scribble and said, "It says, 'I got mine. You get yours.'" (money)

1233. "I got to thinking, you know, the way you do when the TV is on the fritz." (Roseann Barrr)

1234. Q. What tables can you eat?

A. Vege <u>tables.</u>

1235. A man was trying to make a date with a lady he'd just met in a bar. They were sitting on adjacent bar stools.. The woman finally asked him, "Are you married?"

He hesitated, and then he said, "Why, yes I am."

The woman told him, "Well, you go home to your wife. I don't fool around with married men."

"Well, neither does she," the man replied.

1236. Q. What did the vampire call his parents?

A. Deady and Mummy.

1237. Q. Why did he elephant miss the circus rain?

A. It took too long to pack his trunk.

1238.   Q. What do you get when you put your car in a big oven? A. A hot rod.

1239.   Q. What do they call recently married dandelions?

A. Newly weeds.

1240.   A man, upon leaving a restaurant, went to the hat check counter. He began arguing with the hat check girl. "Hey, I left my hat here. Where is it?"

The girl replied, "Sir, I'm sure you were empty headed when you came in here."

1241.   Here's a World War II joke. A woman in Berlin had a restaurant business. She always gave generous servings of food. One day, a member of the Gestapo visited and told her, "You've got to give smaller servings. There's a food shortage."

She put a sign in her window—BECAUSE OF HESS, I AM SERVING LESS.

Another Gestapo man visited and said, "Your servings are still too large. You've got to cut down"

She put another sign in her window, "BECAUSE OF HITLER, I AM SERVING LITTLER.

Another Gestapo man visited and told her, "You've got to make your servings much smaller."

She made another sign to put in the window: CLOSED. BECAUSE OF GORING, I HVE RETURNED TO MY PREVIOUS PROFESSION.

1242.   Knock knock.

Who's there?

Dwayne.

Dwayne who?

Dwayne the tub. I'm dwonding.

1243. Q. Why are automatic transmissions bad for you?

A. Because they make you shiftless.

1244. Q. What day of the week do fish hate?

A Fridays. (Fry days)

1245. Q. What did one potato chip say to another chip?

A. Let's go for a dip.

1246. Q. Why does George work as a baker?

A. He kneads he dough. (needs)

1247. Q. When you were in school, didn't you lean the three Rs? A. Yeah. Rah! Rah! Rah!

1248. Q. What did the priest say when he saw a cow walking down the aisle of a church?

A. Holy Cow!

1249. Q. What did one casket say to another casket?

A. Is that you coughing? (coffin)

1250. You can find out a lot about other people by what they say about you.

1251. Did you hear about the man who was so stupid he thought that "Moby Dick" was a venereal disease?

1252. People are like stained glass windows. In daylight, they shine like brilliant jewels. But at night, they shine only if they have an inner radiance.

1253. Q. When crossing the Delaware River, why did George Washington stand up in the boat?

A. Because if he had sat down, they would have given him an oar.

1254. Q. What's the book about cars called?

A. An Auto Biography. (autobiography)

1255. Q. Why do dragons sleep in the daytime?

A. So they can fight knights (nights)

1256. Q. Why did the scientist cross a centipede with a turkey?

A. So everyone could have a drumstick for Thanksgiving.

1257. Dick: "Hey Tom, you've got a Yale pennant on your wall up here above the fireplace. Did you really go to Yale?"

Dick: "No. I didn't actually go there, but I have their locks on all my doors?"

Q. Where's Harry?

A. He stayed at home because he did not want to get mixed up in all this foolishness.

1258. Student: "Say, Mr. Jones, I was thinking of becoming a teacher. Is there a course I should take to prepare myself?"

Just then an apple was thrown at the teacher's head.

Teacher: "Yes. KARATE!"

1259. A man was sitting reading his newspaper when his wife hit him on the head with a flyswatter.

"What's that for?" the man asked.

The wife replied, "That was for the piece of paper with the name Jenny on it that I found in your pants pocket."

The man then said, "When I was at the races last week, Jenny was the name of the horse I bet on..

The wife apologized and went on cleaning windows.

Three days later while the man was watching TV, his wife hit him again with a flyswatter.

He said, "Hey, what's wrong with you?

She said calmly, "Your horse Jenny phoned today."

1260. A man was telling his neighbor, "I just bought a new hearing aid. It cost me four thousand dollars, but it is state of the art. It's perfect.

"Really," answered the neighbor. "What kind is it?"

"Twelve thirty." (Kind sounds like time, for a person hard of hearing.)

1261. An elderly man was invited by his old friend, an Army buddy, for dinner one evening. He was impressed by the way his buddy preceded every request to his wife with endearing terms—Honey, My Love, Darling, Sweetheart, Pumpkin, etc. The couple had been married almost 7 0 years, and clearly they appeared to be very much in love.

While the wife was in the kitchen, the man leaned over and said, ""I think it's wonderful that, after all these years, you still call our wife those loving pet names."

The old Army buddy hung his head and whispered, "I have to tell you the truth. I forgot her name ten years ago."

1262. Teacher: "Tell me, Tommy, if I had 9 apples and there were 12 children, how would I divide them equally?"

Tommy: "Make applesauce."

1263. Dad: "Son, I want you to have something I never had in school. Son: "What's that?"

Dad: "Passing grades."

1264. Girl: "I had to slap my boyfriend's face three times at the drive-in last night."

Friend: "Why? Did he try to kiss you?"

Girl: "No. He kept falling asleep and I wanted to wake him up."

1265. Old lady: "I had to slap that old man who took me to the movies. I had to slap him five times."

Old lady's friend: "But why? You said you wanted to see a little action."

Old lady: "I did. He was so spaced out I thought he was dead."

1266. Litle boy: "Mom, how come most of the angels don't have whiskers?"

Mom: "That's because most of the angels are women. They don't have beards to shave."

Little boy: "But what about the men? Doesn't God let men go to heaven?

MOM: "Very few men go to heaven. And, if they do, it's by a very close shave."

1267. Q. What's a bankrupt baker?"

A. That's a guy with no dough.

1268. A feeble old man was sitting by himself in a busy restaurant. Finally a young waitress asked, "What will you have sir?"

He replied, "A few kind words and a bowl of soup."

The waitress leaned down close to his ear and whispered, "Don't eat the soup."

1269. Q. Why is the funeral business so profitable?

A. Because people are just dying to get in.

1270. A funeral director wanted to increase his business. So, he asked his teen-age son for a suggestion. The son said, "Let's change the name. Smith's Funeral Home sounds ho-hum."

At breakfast the next morning, the father asked his teen-age son, "Did you think of a name?"

"Yeah, I did. You need something jazzier! How about CADAVERS ARE US?"

1271.   Q. Where does Friday come before Monday?

A. In the dictionary?

1272.   Q. There were five people under one umbrella. Why didn't they get wet?

A. It wasn't raining.

1273.   Q. Where do cows go when they want a night out?

A. To the Moooovies

Girl: Where are we going?

Boy: Let's movie. (Changing a noun into a verb!)

1274.   Here's one for only the teacher's eyes:

Q. What can you do with 65 used condoms?

A. Make them into a tire and call it a GOOD YEAR.

1275.   Joe: "Can a pig drive a car?"

Moe: "Yep. Have you heard of a road hog?"

BOOKS BY STANLEY B. GRAHAM

COUNTRY ZOO: The Perils of a First-Year Teacher (a novel) -- Out of Print. After reprinting the price

Will be $15.00.

MEDITATIONS OF A GREAT LAKES SAILOR (a novel) -- $15.00

PORTRAIT OF A LADY: The Biography of Elizabeth-Ramirez-Graham -- $15.00

THE NEXT TRAIN TO CHICAGO: The Story of the Life and Loves of a Century Woman (a novel)$15.00

THE CIVIL WAR DIARY OF LOUIS M. ALBRIGHT -- $20.00

I WAS HERE: The Young Manhood and Education of Rick Stevens -- $25.00

TO BECOME A RICH AMERICAN (a novel) -- $25.00

A FAREWELL TO THREE WIVES: The Marriages of Rick Stevens -- $25.00

TEACHER'S JOKE & STORY BOOK -- Collected by Stanley B. Graham $13.99

If you would like to buy one or more books, please fill out this order form and mail it with your check to Belding Publishing. If you buy two books, you will receive a $10.00 discount. If you buy three books, you will receive a $20.00 discount If you wish to purchase more than three books (perhaps using them as gifts), there will be a discount of $10.00 for each additional book. There is no charge for shipping and handling.

Please print or use an address label.

NAME_____

STREET ADDRESS_____

CITY_____STATE_____ZIP _____

_____ copy (copies) of (Title) _____Price _____

_____ copy (copies) of (Title) _____Price _____

_____ copy (copies) of (Title) _____Price _____

_____ copy (copies) of (Title) _____Price _____

_____ copy (copies) of (Title) _____Price _____

Total (before discount) $ _____

Minus Discount of $10.00, $20.00 etc. - $ _____

Total (after discount) $ _____

Please make checks payable to: Belding Publishing
                                 Bradley Court
                                 Medina, Ohio 44256

Printed in the United States
By Bookmasters